D0619566

The Music Industry, 2nd edition

Digital Media and Society Series

The Music Industry: Music in the Cloud, 2nd edition

PATRIK WIKSTRÖM

polity

Copyright © Patrik Wikström 2013

The right of Patrik Wikström to be identified as Author of this Work has been asserted in accordance with the UK Copyright, Designs and Patents Act 1988.

First published in 2013 by Polity Press.

Polity Press
65 Bridge Street
Cambridge CB2 1UR, UK

Polity Press
350 Main Street
Malden, MA 02148, USA

All rights reserved. Except for the quotation of short passages for the purpose of criticism and review, no part of this publication may be reproduced, stored in a retrieval system, or transmitted, in any form or by any means, electronic, mechanical, photocopying, recording or otherwise, without the prior permission of the publisher.

ISBN-13: 978-0-7456-6417-0
ISBN-13: 978-0-7456-6418-7(pb)

A catalogue record for this book is available from the British Library.

Typeset in 10.25 on 13 pt FF Scala
by Servis Filmsetting Ltd, Stockport, Cheshire
Printed in Great Britain by TJ International Ltd, Padstow, Cornwall

The publisher has used its best endeavours to ensure that the URLs for external websites referred to in this book are correct and active at the time of going to press. However, the publisher has no responsibility for the websites and can make no guarantee that a site will remain live or that the content is or will remain appropriate.

Every effort has been made to trace all copyright holders, but if any have been inadvertently overlooked the publisher will be pleased to include any necessary credits in any subsequent reprint or edition.

For further information on Polity, visit our website: www.politybooks.com

ACC LIBRARY SERVICES AUSTIN, TX

For Pia

Contents

Tables and Figures

Tables

Figures

Acknowledgements

First I would like to thank all the informants whom I have interviewed over the years. Your thoughts are at the centre of this work and without your involvement the project would not have been conceivable. I would also like to send thanks to my students, colleagues in academia and friends in the industry for helping me shape this book by giving me inspiration, encouragement and criticism along the way.

Introduction:
Music in the Cloud

One Sunday in early March 2008, the industrial rock megastar Trent Reznor, a.k.a. Nine Inch Nails, released his seventh studio project, *Ghosts I–IV*. The project consisted in total of 36 instrumental songs recorded during 10 weeks in the autumn of 2007. Even though Nine Inch Nails was a global brand and Trent Reznor had millions of devoted fans all over the world, he was at the time without a contract with a major record label after having ended a relationship with the Universal label, Interscope Records. 'As of right now Nine Inch Nails is a totally free agent, free of any recording contract with any label', Reznor wrote on the band's website. 'I have been under recording contracts for 18 years and have watched the business radically mutate from one thing to something inherently very different and it gives me great pleasure to be able to finally have a direct relationship with the audience as I see fit and appropriate.' For *Ghosts I–IV*, Reznor decided that the appropriate distribution channel would be the official Nine Inch Nails website 'nin.com'. He also chose to release the songs under a licence that allowed fans to remix and redistribute the work in a multitude of different formats (cf. p. 179). On 13 March, Reznor launched the second phase of the project. First, multitrack versions of a number of songs from *Ghosts* were added to the remix section of 'nin.com' where fans could upload their own remixes, listen to and review the remixes from other fans, vote for their favourites, and so on. Second, Reznor launched an Internet-based 'Film Festival' on YouTube where he invited fans to create and upload their visual interpretations of the songs. The fans' reception of the *Ghosts* project cannot be labelled as anything but exceptional. By the end of 2008 fans had uploaded more than 2,000 videos to the Film Festival, and an unknown but large number of user-generated remixes had been posted to 'remix.nin.com'. Besides remixing and uploading the tracks from *Ghosts I–IV*, fans were also able to download nine of the original songs for free from the website. They were also offered four other product packages, ranging from a '$5 Download' which included all 36 songs in various formats to a '$300 Ultra Deluxe Limited Edition Package' which included downloads, CDs, DVDs and glossy booklets, all signed by Reznor himself. According to Reznor, during the first week after the launch 781,917 transactions generated $1,619,420 in sales revenue. In addition, the '$5 Download' version was released on Amazon MP3 Downloads and remained as one of their top-selling albums, at least during March and April 2008.[1] It is notable that this result was achieved while the album, in its entirety, obviously also was available via various illegal file-sharing networks and services.

A few years later, in September 2012, Trent Reznor announced that his band How to Destroy Angels had signed with the Sony Music label, Columbia Records, to release a number of their upcoming albums (Reznor 2012). Reznor concluded in a Facebook post that 'complete independent releasing has its great points but also comes with shortcomings'. It remains to be seen if this move marks the end of Reznor's experiments in the DIY sphere, or if the How to Destroy Angels project requires a major label treatment in order to reach mainstream audiences via terrestrial radio. Nevertheless, and even though Reznor's *Ghosts I–IV* stands out as a rather extraordinary case, it beautifully encapsulates the music industry about a decade after Shawn Fanning[2] released Napster and peer-to-peer file-sharing to the masses and changed the music industry forever. The structure of the *Ghosts I–IV* project is fundamentally different compared to the twentieth-century music industry model where vertically integrated multinational music companies control how, when and where their albums are released, promoted and distributed. The core of the *Ghosts I–IV* project is not the set of tracks

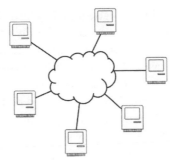

Figure 0.1   The Cloud as an Internet metaphor

recorded in Reznor's recording studio in the outskirts of Beverly Hills. Rather, it is Reznor's relationship with his fans and in the thousands of remixes, videos, comments and blog posts uploaded to nin.com, YouTube, ninremixes.com and a host of other more or less shady places in the Cloud.

'The Cloud' has been used as a metaphor to denote the Internet since the late 1960s and early 1970s, when Vinton Cerf, Robert Kahn, Robert Metcalfe, Leonard Kleinrock, Larry Roberts and many others invented the technologies behind the network of networks. A cloud was considered to be a useful and vague enough symbol that could be used to summarize all the resources, cables and gadgets connecting the computers at the nodes of the network (Figure 0.1). These days, 'The Cloud' is still used as a metaphor for the Internet, but it also conveys other meanings. For more than 20 years, the computer company Sun Microsystems (acquired in 2010 by Oracle) pushed the slogan 'The Network is the Computer'. Sun suggested back in those days that the resources in the Cloud would soon become so powerful that the computers at the network nodes would no longer have to be sophisticated and expensive but could be made extremely simple and cheap. Eventually, technology did not choose exactly that path, but, in some respects, what during recent years has been promoted as 'Web 2.0' to a large extent is based on the basic principles suggested by Sun. Web 2.0 is a term that is usually employed to denote a family of Web-based services which are far more complex than the traditional, relatively static information-based Web pages. Web 2.0 services are really fully-fledged Web-based software systems which enable users to socialize with friends and family, store and edit photos, listen to and remix music and many other things. For instance, in the area of productivity software, Web 2.0 services make it possible for users to subscribe to word-processing, spreadsheets, email, calendars and similar resources, rather than having to purchase the traditional Office package from Microsoft (see, e.g., Carr 2008).

In this book, I apply the concept of the Cloud to the field of music to emphasize how the music industry has completely shifted its centre of gravity from the physical to the virtual – from the Disk to the Cloud. Many years have passed since young party-goers relied on CDs for music, and today it is also less common to play MP3s stored on their computers or iPods. Instead, increasingly, they listen to music from YouTube, last. fm, Pandora, Spotify, remix.nin.com, or some other Web-based music service; or they download a party mix from a file-sharing network such as BitComet or LimeWire. Music is no longer something that mainstream audiences own and collect – music is in the Cloud.

The purpose of this book is to explore the transformation of the music industry as manifested by projects such as *Ghosts I– IV*. Of course, it is not the first time the music industry has been transformed by changes in the media environment. Changes in broadcast radio programming during the 1950s, the compact cassette during the 1970s and the deregulation of media ownership during the 1990s all had a tremendous impact on the structure and logic of the industry. However, the transformation that took place during the first decade of the twenty-first century is even more dramatic than the previous ones. Certainly, as I will stress in this book, there are many aspects of the old music industry that remain the same, regardless of whether the music is on the Disk or in the Cloud. However, the transformation is of such magnitude that it is relevant to talk about a 'new' music industry dynamics or a 'new music economy', as it sometimes has been referred to (D'Arcangelo 2007; Denis 2008; Goodman 2008). But what are the basic features of such a 'new music economy'? I argue that three tensions or dimensions are fundamental in order to understand this phenomenon. I choose to refer to these as 'connectivity vs. control', 'service vs. product' and 'amateur vs. professional'.

Connectivity vs. control

In order to make a living in the old music economy it was all about control – a music firm's top priority was to maximize the revenues from each individual piece of intellectual property and to minimize unauthorized use. In the new music economy, it is still important to know how the audience uses intellectual property but it is more or less impossible to regulate and police that use. I borrow a term from network theory – connectivity – to explain the new situation. Connectivity is a measure of how well the members of a network are connected. A network is considered to have a high level of connectivity if most of its members are connected to each other, and vice versa. In Figure 0.2, the network to the left has lower connectivity than the network to the right. In a network with high connectivity, information, money, fads, norms, etc. easily flow between the members (see, e.g., Watts 2003).

In the old music economy, the network constituted by music companies and audiences had a relatively low level of connectivity. Basically, there were strong connections running between the music firms and the audience, but only weak connections between individual members of the audience (illustrated by the left network in Figure 0.2). Consequently, the music firms could control the flow of music with relative ease, since there was nothing to link the different elements that made up the audience.

In the new music economy, the importance of physical music

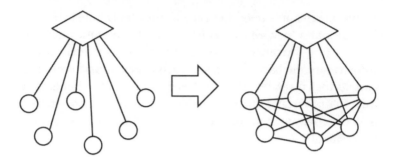

Figure 0.2   Increased connectivity causes the music firms to lose their ability to control the flow of information

distribution and mass media has been radically reduced, while the importance of Internet media has exploded. These new communication technologies have an entirely different structure from the previous hierarchical media. The technologies lower the barriers, which had previously restricted the capability to distribute information to the network, i.e. the capability to upload information to the Cloud. Now, the capability to upload is theoretically accessible to everyone connected to the network. As a consequence, the connectivity of the 'audience–music firm' network has increased, which in turn has resulted in the music firms losing their ability to control the flow of information. In a nutshell, the new music industry dynamics is characterized by high connectivity and little control.

Service vs. product

In the old music economy, the content (music) and the medium (disk) were inseparable, and the music industry clearly was an industry made up of physical goods. In the new music economy, characterized by high connectivity and little control, it becomes increasingly difficult to charge a premium for discrete chunks of information. As soon as some kind of information is uploaded to the Cloud, it is instantly universally accessible to everyone connected to the Cloud. In such a 'friction-free network',[3] the economic value of providing access to an individual track is infinitesimally close to zero.

But there are other things that remain chargeable. In a world where information is abundant, people may not be willing to pay a premium for basic access to that information, but they are most likely willing to pay for services which help them navigate through the vast amounts of information. If music is thought of as a service, it is possible to fathom consumer propositions that are both valuable to the audience and respectful to the work of the creative artists. More on that later in this book.

Amateur vs. professional

The role of the creative artist is the most respected and admired in the music industrial ecosystem. Nine Inch Nails, Regina Spektor, Stevie Wonder, Céline Dion: all are powerful brands that appeal to millions of fans all over the world. I praise these extraordinarily talented individuals and recognize their work as the music industry's centre of gravity. However, in the new music economy, the relationship between these brands, their art and the audience has changed. The increased connectivity of the audience network combined with various kinds of music production tools enable 'non-professionals' to create, remix and publish content online. This does not necessarily imply that, in the new music economy, every music listener is also an amateur musician, but nevertheless a considerable share of the audience does create and upload content to the Cloud. For instance, research into the world of fan fiction shows that approximately 5 per cent of a user population creates and uploads content, 12 per cent comments on that content and 24 per cent actively reads the content and the comments (Olin-Scheller & Wikström 2009). Bradley Horowitz, vice-president at Google and formerly vice-president at Yahoo!, reports similar results from studies of user behaviour at Yahoo! Groups (Horowitz 2006). It is not entirely unrealistic to assume that those fans who create, remix and upload content are also the most dedicated and loyal. It is also quite likely that they are the ones who spend the most on concerts, merchandise, etc. Based on those two assumptions, it makes sense for music firms to secure a good relationship with this section of the audience, encourage their creative desires and do their best not to push them away.

To sum up: the new music industry dynamics is characterized by high connectivity and little control; music provided as a service; and increased amateur creativity. The driver of all these changes is primarily the development of digital information and communication technologies. The music industry started its journey into the 'digital age' a long time ago, during the 1970s, when digital technologies were introduced in the areas of music production and recording. During the 1980s, primarily due to the introduction of the compact disk, the use of these technologies expanded to music distribution. Lastly, during the late 1990s and early 2000s, Internet technologies became the most important drivers of change, and ultimately brought every remaining part of the music business, including promotion and talent development, into the realm of digital technology.

The number of technological innovations related to this third period of change has literally exploded: BitTorrent, Facebook, iTunes/iPod, Qtrax, SoundCloud, last.fm, LimeWire, MySpace, MOG, Rhapsody, Pandora, Spotify, Rdio, are only a few out of an overwhelming number of music technology brands. Although many of these innovations may be relevant as markers of the new music industry dynamics, this book does not analyse the details of any such specific innovation. My ambition is rather to stay above the level of these 'technological ripples' and try to discern the long-term patterns that are created by the innovations in aggregate.

During this period of change I have been able to meet a large number of music industry professionals and to discuss with them their understanding of the new dynamics. I use quotes from these interviews to illustrate and strengthen the reasoning.

In order to ensure the anonymity of the informants, I conceal their identities in relation to their quotes and introduce them by their profession – for example 'product manager' or 'producer'. I conducted interviews with professionals from the US, the UK and Sweden. Why these countries, one might ask? The UK and the US warrant the attention of this study since they constitute two of the largest and most influential national music markets in the world (IFPI 2012a), in terms of both consumption and production. Sweden is a much smaller market than the other two, but a nation with a 'fantastically rich music culture' (BBC News 2006) and a history as a strong exporter of popular music (see, e.g., ExMS 2005). Sweden is also interesting since it is a country with an advanced information technology infrastructure and a copyright legislation that has been slow to adapt to international treaties (Keller 2006). This combination has nurtured an environment, which has established Sweden as 'a haven for copyright infringement' (BBC News 2006; Reuters 2006).

This study does not try to explain any differences between the behaviour of the three markets. Rather, it focuses on the similarities between the three. When certain behaviour is seen to occur in all three markets, it is assumed to be indicating that the dynamics is of significance and should be included in the overall reasoning. The term 'the music industry' is often used in the text, and is formally a reference to the national music industries in the three countries included in the study. However, the music industry is one of the copyright industries in which national borders are of only minor significance. Most markets are dominated by a handful of multinational organizations, and, thus, innovations, practices, people and routines easily flow across national borders. It may consequently be possible to extend the validity of the findings presented by this study beyond the three countries. At least the European Union and North America could be included, and perhaps also the other members of the OECD. Finally, it should be noted that the three markets are examined on a national level only and no attention is paid to the dynamics of local markets within each territory.

The structure of the book

This is a book about the Cloud-based music industry. I argue that this industry is characterized by high connectivity and little control; music provided as a service; and increased amateur creativity.

In chapter 1, I start out by labelling the music industry as a 'copyright industry'. I discuss characteristics and features that distinguish these industries from other, 'non-copyright industries'. I then pay attention to the debate about the possible tension between profit maximization and creativity. Lastly, I present my theoretical platform, which is based on frameworks from organizational theory, social learning theory and the sociology of culture.

In the second chapter, I turn the attention to the inside of the music industry. It is important to understand the workings of the traditional music industry in order to recognize the significance of the change that has created the new music industry dynamics. I therefore use well-established models to explain and discuss the music industry and its three sub-sectors: recorded music, music publishing and live music. I give an account of the history of the industry and present some basic facts about a number of multinational organizations that at the time of writing can be considered as the industry's most dominant players.

After having introduced and contextualized the music industry, I use the next three chapters to analyse different aspects of the transformation of the industry. In chapter 3, I analyse the relationship between recorded music, media and audiences. I start out by presenting a model of this relationship used to support an analysis of the changes in the media environment. I focus on how the increased connectivity of the audience–music firm network shapes the new music economy and I introduce concepts such as 'audience fragmentation' and 'option value blurring'. This part of the analysis is particularly focused on the recorded music sector and the music licensing sector. In the area of music licensing, I examine the changing roles of music publishing and the music publisher in the new music industry dynamics. In the area of the recorded music sector, I focus on a range of new business models, which have been developed by music business entrepreneurs. I examine the models' viability in the light of the shifting levels of connectivity and control and discuss the concept of music as a service.

Chapter 4 is focused on music-making. I have already noted in this introduction that one of the most important characteristics of the new music economy is the rise of amateur creativity and the increase of so-called user-generated content. However, in chapter 4, I will focus on the professional making of music, both in the studio and on stage. I explore the changes in the production system of popular music, primarily related to the roles and careers of songwriters, artists and producers, and to the changes in the institutions and structures of that system.

In chapter 5, I focus on the role of music fans, and how this affects every aspect of the new music economy, including distribution, promotion, production and talent development. I examine how fans' desire to listen to music, use music and express themselves through music is sometimes in conflict with copyright legislation.

Finally I take the discussion into the future and reflect on how the trends of today will shape the music industry of tomorrow.

1

A Copyright Industry

In this chapter I argue that the contemporary music industry is best understood as a 'copyright industry'. I explain why this is an important starting point in the digital age and argue for the necessity of this shift in perspective. I then develop a theoretical platform based on frameworks from organizational theory, social learning theory and the sociology of culture.

Defining industries

Most scholars, regardless of discipline, try to classify and label the objects they research. Music industry scholars do not deviate from this norm, and during the development of the field the music industry has been categorized as a 'creative industry', an 'experience industry' and a 'cultural industry', to name but a few. In this section I examine some of these labels, and I also say why I prefer to use the term 'copyright industry'.

The oldest label, the 'culture industry', is usually traced back to the Frankfurt School of Critical Theory and its most recognized scholars, Max Horkheimer and Theodor Adorno. Between 1935 and 1949 the research institute was relocated to Columbia University in New York, and it was during this period that Horkheimer and Adorno wrote their most important work, the *Dialektik der Aufklärung* (1944).[4] In this very influential and pessimistic book, the authors outline how the world is moving closer to self-destruction. One of the chapters examines the 'culture industry', which, it is argued, is the result of a process whereby an increase in media and communication technologies leads to the industrial production, circulation and consumption of cultural commodities. The industrialization of these processes results in formulaic, standardized, repetitive, pre-digested products, which reduce the audience to a 'child-like' state (Adorno 1941; Hesmondhalgh 2002; Horkheimer & Adorno 1944; Negus 1996, 1997).

During the 1970s, French scholars (e.g., Miège 1979) and policymakers (e.g., Girard 1981) decided to pick up the term. However, they also decided to revise its meaning considerably. First, they changed its form from singular to plural (cultural industries) to denote the diversity between different cultural industries. Second, they rejected the pessimistic and nostalgic position assumed by the Frankfurt School. Instead, they argued that the commodification of culture, facilitated by new technologies, also had its positive sides. For instance, the new technologies enabled innovation and, in addition, ordinary people were allowed access to culture that had previously been out of their reach. Third, while Horkheimer and Adorno considered the field of popular, industrialized culture as frozen and static, these scholars argued that the cultural industries represent a dynamic zone of continuing struggle between commerce and art (Hesmondhalgh 2002: 15–17; Towse 2001: 25).

The early definitions of cultural industries and cultural products are not radically different from today. Hirsch defined cultural products as 'nonmaterial goods directed at a public of consumers, for whom they generally serve an aesthetic or expressive, rather than utilitarian function' (1972: 641) Three decades later, the definitions suggested by scholars such as Throsby (2001) and Hesmondhalgh (2002) were very similar to Hirsch's explanation. Hesmondhalgh, for instance, considers the cultural industries as 'industries based upon the industrial production and circulation of texts, and which are centrally reliant on the work of symbol creators' (2002: 14).

Hesmondhalgh's definition requires two comments. First, regarding the interpretation of the term 'text'. All cultural artefacts could be considered as texts. However, some cultural artefacts can be mainly functional (e.g., cars, clothes, furniture) while others are mainly communicative (e.g., songs, images, stories, performances). In his definition of cultural industries, Hesmondhalgh is only referring to the latter, that is to say texts that are mainly communicative or symbolic in their nature (2002: 12). Second, instead of using the term 'artist', Hesmondhalgh uses the term 'symbol creators' for those who make up, interpret or rework these texts (2002: 4–5).

When explicitly defining which industries are cultural and which are not, Girard (1981) suggested that broadcasting, publishing, music and film should be included. Hesmondhalgh's list of 'core cultural industries' is similar to Girard's, but with the addition of advertising and interactive media (Hesmondhalgh 2002: 12).[5] Girard did actually consider advertising as one of the cultural industries, and it is quite understandable why in 1981 he did not choose to add interactive media to the list.

The term 'cultural industries' is a rather appealing label with several strengths. The term has a long heritage and has been widely accepted by scholars. However, the term has also been criticized. For instance, Cunningham (2005) argues that 'cultural industries' is an out-dated term that is linked to analogue media, nationalistic cultural policies, neoclassical economics applied to the arts, etc. Several other alternative terms aimed at defining the same industries (including the music industry) have therefore been suggested. In policy circles, terms such as 'creative industries' and 'experience industries' have become widely popular. These definitions usually have a wider scope than the original term and include industries or activities such as architecture, design, fashion, performing arts, crafts and sometimes even tourism, sport and restaurants.

These newer concepts have radically changed the relationship between government and culture. As Hartley describes it:

> The 'creative industries' idea brought creativity from the back door of government, where it had sat for decades holding out the tin cup for arts subsidy . . . to the front door, where it was introduced to the wealth-creating portfolios, the emergent industry departments, and the enterprise support programs.

> . . . Creative industries [helped] revitalize cities and regions that had moved out of heavy industry, had never developed a strong manufacturing base or who were over-exposed to declining IT industries. (2005: 19)

Manchester and Liverpool in the UK are two examples of such governmental reform initiatives (O'Connor 2000). This focus on regional development has also led to an increased interest in these industries by economic geography scholars (e.g., Hallencreutz 2002; Leyshon 2001; Power 2003). In addition, the mapping of these industries has turned into a lucrative business for scholars and consultants alike. Many regions and nations decide they need healthy creative industries and, in order to achieve that goal, the definition of what is actually a part of these industries differs from nation to nation and region to region. For instance, pundits and policymakers in Sweden have decided to use the term 'experience industry', which also includes tourism and restaurants. These two sectors combined account for almost 40 per cent of the entire 'experience industry' in Sweden and make the definition quite incompatible with many other nations' industry definitions (Almqvist & Dahl 2003).

The term 'experience industry' stems from Pine and Gilmore (1998) and, according to the creators, it may include many business sectors, including retailing, transportation, tourism, banking, media, etc. Pine and Gilmore did not use the term experience industry, but referred to the 'experience economy'. The experience economy emphasizes how an activity is executed rather than what that activity is all about. The term 'creative industries' (Caves 2000; Hartley 2005; Howkins 2001) has, since the early 2000s, largely replaced 'cultural industries' as the most frequently used industry label, especially in Anglophone countries. It differs from 'experience industry' since it is not focused on how an activity is executed, but on the input required for that execution. However, the problem with this term is almost the same as with 'experience industry': it is far too inclusive. Most definitions of the creative industries include architecture, design and fashion. The same arguments motivating the inclusion of these industries could be used, for instance, to include the consumer electronics industry, the automotive industry or the pharmaceutical industry, where creativity also is of great importance. The scope of the definition is so wide that any attempt to produce knowledge which has validity across all the industries included becomes a futile endeavour. Proponents of the term answer this criticism by stating that creative processes are found across all industries, and it is not possible to define the 'creative industries' by their output, since it is focused upon the input of these processes (Hartley 2005: 27). That claim is true enough, but industries are not defined by input, or by the manner in which activities are performed. Industries are defined by the goods or services produced or supplied.

It is certainly true that creativity is an important part of many industries, perhaps it is even of growing importance to the entire economy, but, once again, it is questionable whether creativity is a useful label to delineate a part of the economy in order to facilitate structured analysis. The shortcomings of the term 'creative or experience industries' have been recognized by several scholars in the field. There is actually a tendency to link the prefix 'creative' to concepts such as 'economy', 'class' or 'citizen' rather than to 'industry' (see, e.g., Florida 2002; Hartley 2007).

Yet another term that also deserves some attention is the term 'media industries'. Ferguson (2006: 297), Picard (2002: 12–17) and others all give the term a meaning which is very similar to 'cultural industries' but there are nevertheless some minor distinctions between the various definitions. Traditionally, the (mass) media industries include the newspaper, magazine, radio and television industries. However, due to the evolution of these industries, the definition of what is and what is not part of the media industries has been challenged. The 'Internet industry' is now often included, and other scholars choose to include book, film, videogame, music and advertising in the definition (Ferguson 2006; Picard 2002) – in other words, a definition which is almost identical to Hesmondhalgh's listing of the core cultural industries (2002: 12).

The list of suggested terms that might be used to label the music industry continues and includes some fairly exotic terms, such as the 'sunrise industries'. However, rather than using any of the terms discussed above, I believe a useful way to categorize the music industry is to consider it as a copyright industry. Copyright legislation is what makes it possible to commodify a musical work, be it a song, an arrangement, a recording, etc. The core of the music industry is about 'developing musical content and personalities' (Negus 1992), and, to be able to license the use of that content, they need to be protected by copyright legislation.

The use of this term is not new in any way, but has been used by several institutions, for instance OECD (2005), IFPI (2004a), Congress of the United States (CBO 2004) and of course by the WIPO. I argue that by considering the music industry as a copyright industry rather than a cultural or a creative industry, I emphasize the nature of the products that are created and traded within that industry. The term also has a clearer definition and is less ambiguous than many of the other terms, which makes it more useful during analyses of the dynamics of these firms and industries.

Now, when I have categorized the music industry as a copyright industry, a number of important questions need to be addressed, such as: What features characterize this kind of industry? What is known about the behaviour of the copyright industry? What approach should be used in order to be able to explain the dynamics of these industries in the digital age? Let us first start with the basic concepts of copyright.

Basic concepts of copyright

The Statute of Anne (named after Queen Anne) is generally considered to be the world's earliest copyright legislation. This English law, which went into force in 1710, marks a shift from a system where printers were able to print books without compensating the authors for their creative labour to a system where *authors* would have the exclusive right to reproduce books. The Act explains its background and purpose:

> Whereas Printers, Booksellers, and other Persons, have of late frequently taken the Liberty of Printing, Reprinting, and Publishing, or causing to be Printed, Reprinted, and Published Books, and other Writings, without the Consent of the Authors or Proprietors of such Books and Writings, to their very great Detriment, and too often to the Ruin of them and their Families: For Preventing therefore such Practices for the future, and for the Encouragement of Learned Men to Compose and Write useful Books.

The copyright legislation was from the beginning a national law that only covered literary works, but over the centuries it was expanded to include paintings, drawings, music, etc. It was also widened to provide protection not only for a nation's own artists but for all artists, regardless of their origin and nationality. The most important legislation in international copyright law is the Berne Convention, adopted in 1886. It was the French author Victor Hugo who was the strongest proponent for recognizing authors' rights internationally, which eventually resulted in the Berne Convention. Over the years, the Convention has been developed and expanded in order to recognize a number of copyright-related features which now are considered as fundamental and crucial in international copyright legislation – for instance, that no formalities shall be required in order for there to be a copyright; in other words, it is not necessary to register a song for it to be protected (Article 5: Rights Guaranteed). Since 1948, the Convention has also governed 'additional rights' in order to respond to new technologies, such as sound recording technology (Article 9: Right of Reproduction). The Berne Convention also introduced the concept of moral rights – that is, the right to be recognized as author, and for one's work not to be subject to derogatory treatment:

> Independently of the author's economic rights, and even after the transfer of the said rights, the author shall have the right to claim authorship of the work and to object to any distortion,

mutilation or other modification of, or other derogatory action in relation to, the said work, which would be prejudicial to his honor or reputation. (The Berne Convention – Article 6bis: Moral Rights)

The moral right is an example of how copyright-related legislation differs between countries, even though it is international. In many countries with a 'civil law legal system' (which is the predominant legal system in the world), the right to be recognized as the author of a creative work is an inalienable right – it cannot be transferred, bought or sold. This is often not the case in countries with a 'common law legal system' (primarily nations which trace their legal heritage to Britain, including the UK, the US and other former colonies of the British Empire). In these countries, the moral right is considered to be similar to the copyright and can be bought or sold like any other commodity. The regulatory differences between countries have implications for contracts signed between parties in the music industry, and any other copyright industry for that matter. In some countries, moral rights can be covered by the contract, while in other countries they cannot. In order to cope with this 'difficulty' in civil law countries, it is common for artists to agree not to enforce their moral rights, even if they do formally still have them.

The Berne Convention was originally a European instrument, but since 1989, when the USA signed the Convention, and since 1994, when the TRIPS (Trade-Related Aspects of Intellectual Property Rights) Agreement made the Convention a mandatory part of general international trade agreements, the Convention has confirmed its position as the most significant treaty within the realm of international copyright (MacQueen et al. 2007: 38).

The significance of international copyright legislation continues to grow as society moves further into the digital age. New treaties are signed and copyright legislation is one of the most discussed and controversial areas of international law. Among the important treaties that have come into force in recent decades is the 1996 World International Property Organization's

Internet Treaty. This treaty served as the basis for national and regional legislation such as the Digital Millennium Copyright Act (DMCA) in the USA and the European Union Copyright Directive (EUCD) in Europe, which will be further discussed in chapter 5. Another controversial treaty within the European Union is the Directive on the Enforcement of Intellectual Property Rights (IPRED), which came into force during 2004.

Characteristics of the copyright industries

There are several characteristics of the copyright industries that make them distinct from 'non-copyright' industries (see, e.g., Caves 2000: 2–10; Chan-Olmsted 2006: 173; Hesmondhalgh 2002). Some of these characteristics will be discussed in this section.

On the nature of copyright products
As I noted earlier in this chapter, Hirsch defined cultural products as 'nonmaterial goods directed at a public of consumers, for whom they generally serve an aesthetic or expressive, rather than utilitarian function' (1972: 641). In addition to being 'nonmaterial', cultural products have some specific properties that differentiate them from products traded in many other industries.

First of all, the products traded in copyright industries are often categorized as information goods simply because they are intangible and 'can be digitized' (Shapiro & Varian 1999: 3). It is important to note what actually is traded on copyright markets. When people purchase a vase or a CD, they do not purchase the design of the vase or the copyrights to the sound recording. The only thing purchased is an example of the vase design or a right to listen to the sound recording within certain carefully defined restrictions. Only very few are able actually to own music, since full and exclusive copyright of a single commercially successful song is most likely far beyond the financial constraints of the average consumer.

The agreement between the rights holder and the consumer governs how the latter party is allowed to use, for instance, a sound recording. This degree of freedom is often referred to as the product's 'option value' (Shapiro & Varian 1999). If an information product has a high option value, the restrictions on the consumers' ability to use the product are relatively relaxed, and vice versa. A rented DVD has a lower option value than a purchased DVD. A song distributed via broadcast radio has lower option value than a song distributed on a CD or compact cassette.

Copyright products are often referred to as 'experience products' since consumers generally are unable to determine whether a book, film or song is good or not until they have read, seen or heard, respectively (see, e.g., Hoskins & McFadyen 2004: 76–8).[6] Promotion of experience products is often based on the ability to distribute the product with a lower option value. For instance, demo versions of computer software are information goods with limited option value; they are supposed to create a demand for the same product, but with a higher option value. Traditional promotion of popular music is based on the same logic. By playing the song on broadcast radio (low option value), the record company is hoping that a demand is generated for the same information, but with a higher option value – for instance, as distributed via iTunes or on a CD.

Experience products are closely linked to time, basically because it takes time to experience something. The audience also has to make decisions about which copyright products should be awarded their attention. For instance, it is not possible to experience every new song released: there simply isn't enough time. This phenomenon is captured by Herbert Simon's words: 'What information consumes is rather obvious: it consumes the attention of its recipients. Hence, a wealth of information creates a poverty of attention, and a need to allocate that attention efficiently among the overabundance of information sources that might consume it' (1971: 40). The audience is consequently unable to make well-informed decisions regarding its consumption of copyright products. In the case of music, the audience is only able to experience a fraction of the total number of new products released in the market.[7] Compare this, for instance, to the refrigerator market, where consumers are in a much better position to be well informed about the available options. They can compare different retailers' prices and make a rational decision based on solid information. Hirsch describes the completely different situation in the copyright industries: 'In all [such] industries, the number of already available goods far exceeds the number that can be successfully marketed. More goods are produced and available than actually reach the consumer' (1970: 5). In order to cope with this situation, structures have emerged in most copyright industries, which Hirsch refers to as 'preselection systems'. The purpose of the preselection systems is to reduce the number of available products in order to facilitate the audience's decision-making. The preselection system consists of a number of sub-systems, and the members of the different sub-systems, the gatekeepers, determine whether or not the product shall pass through the filtering process.[8]

An industry with a high level of uncertainty and volatility
Many scholars highlight the level of uncertainty and risk in the copyright industries. Negus ponders about uncertainty in the music industry: 'I found much uncertainty among personnel involved in producing music. Neither business executives, fans, the musicians themselves nor journalists can predict what is going to be commercially successful or what new musics are going to be critically acclaimed' (1996: 48). Hirsch also notes how members of a preselection system have limited ability to 'predict accurately which of the items produced will pass successfully through each stage of the complex filter' (1970: 5). Other scholars – for instance, Caves (2000), Hartley (2005), Hoskins & McFadyen (2004) and Picard (2002) – make similar observations.

There are several ways to explain this exceptional condition. First, the development and release of new products, regardless of industry, always involve a high level of risk and uncertainty. In most industries it is difficult to forecast whether a new product will be successful or not. However, the potential success of a copyright product is even more difficult to predict than the success of non-copyright products. If the product category is reasonably well established in the market, consumers might be able to determine whether they would be interested in a new product simply depending on whether or not it fulfils a certain set of criteria. But the consumer can only evaluate a copyright product once 'the first copy' has been produced. Only at that stage is market research of any relevance. Second, the consumption of copyright products is highly volatile and unpredictable (Picard 2002: 7–9). 'Fashionable performers or styles, even if heavily marketed, can suddenly come to be perceived as outmoded, and other texts can become unexpectedly successful' (Hesmondhalgh 2002: 18). Combine these two observations and a situation emerges where it is extremely difficult to gain information about the potential success of a coming release. Consequently, decision-makers in copyright firms often have to base their choices about how to spend their investment monies on intuition and gut feeling. One common way of dealing with such high exposure to risk is to use the principles of portfolio theory (Picard 2002; 2005a; Reca 2006). Risk is reduced by investing in several diverse markets and products in the hope that aggregate return from these investments at least will attain some degree of stability. Hesmondhalgh (2002) refers to this strategy as 'throwing mud' in order to see what sticks. Denisoff (1975) referred to it as 'the buckshot theory' when he explored the music publishing industry. Following this strategy, a considerable number of contracts are signed. By monitoring how consumers react to the songs, the company is able to focus its resources on those products the audiences seem to like.

Following this practice, a staggering amount of new copyright products are released annually. Data on how many new titles (books, music albums, magazines, movies, videogames etc.) are released annually worldwide are not readily available, but at least 1,000,000 books were published worldwide during 2002 (Zaid 2003), and at least 100,000 music albums were released worldwide during 2004 (IFPI 2004b). Hesmondhalgh (2002) refers to Neuman (1991: 139) when claiming that 80 per cent of the revenues in the book publishing industry stems from 20 per cent of the portfolio, and to Wolf (1999: 89) when claiming that only 2 per cent of music albums sold in the US during 1998 sold more than 50,000 copies. In other words, it is this small fraction that supports all the other titles that are unable to deliver acceptable earnings.

High production costs, low reproduction costs
The dominant portion of the costs in copyright industries is attributed to the production of 'the first copy' and the marketing of the title in question. This is to say that, once the first copy or the design has been made, most of the project costs have been paid. Two observations can be made about these costs. First, they are mainly fixed; that is to say, they are independent of the number of products sold. Second, they are usually considered as sunk costs; that is to say; they are paid before the products are available to the public and are not recoverable, even if the project is immediately halted (Hesmondhalgh 2002; Picard 2002; Shapiro & Varian 1999; Vogel 2001).

The cost structure in the copyright industries has considerable effects on the behaviour of copyright firms, primarily because it 'leads to considerable economies of scale, i.e. the more you produce, the lower your average cost of production' (Shapiro & Varian 1999: 21). This means that although a considerable number of items have to be sold before profitability is achieved, the profitability beyond the point of break-even may be substantial. This logic 'leads to a very strong orientation towards audience maximisation in the [copyright] industries' (Hesmondhalgh 2002: 19). In other words, it makes much more economic sense to sell a single title to a large audience than to sell the same number of items, but distributed across 10 different titles.

Profit maximization, creativity and authenticity

An interesting aspect of the copyright industries is the apparent conflict between art and commerce. This section introduces some of the basic concepts related to this debate and links it to the music industrial context.

Firms are economic entities that acquire and organize resources in order to produce goods and services (Picard 2002: 2). According to the neoclassical economic theory usually referred to as the theory of the firm, the objective of a firm is to maximize profit and shareholder value (see, e.g., Hoskins & McFadyen 2004: 141; Picard 2002: 3). Profit is usually defined as 'the money that remains after expenses are subtracted from income' (Picard 2002: 4). Shareholder value is assumed to be created through a combination of share price appreciation and dividends (Knight 1998: 21).

According to this reasoning, economic value is the end, and the activities taking place within the firm are merely means in achieving that end. It does not particularly matter whether those activities generate milkshakes or movies, as long as they deliver profit. While there may be entrepreneurs and managers who subscribe to this perspective, many entrepreneurs in the copyright industries are motivated by something else, beyond profit and economic value (Brulin & Nilsson 1997). The business is an evil necessity, and the creative process, not the profit, is the single and ultimate objective (Karlsson & Lekvall 2002). Regardless of these priorities, there are very few symbol creators who are able to disregard economic realities completely. Any venture has to be able to pay the bills, make improvements in facilities, have access to capital markets, experiment with new methods, and so on; otherwise, the venture will eventually vanish. Most copyright entrepreneurs quickly conclude that a 'firm' is a convenient way to structure their ventures – the practising of their craft. By establishing a firm, they are able to enter business agreements with other economic entities; they are able to compete for external funding for various projects; they can aggregate risk and regulate various uncertainties; they are able to attract talent; and so on (see, e.g., Coase 1937). Consequently, any firm, regardless of whether it is operating in a copyright industry or not, has to deliver some kind of profit. It may be that it is not entirely necessary to maximize profit, but rather to deliver good enough profits that allow the symbol creators to continue practising their craft as long as they are able to keep their spirits burning.

The reasoning above assumes the firm in question is small and that the owners and managers are the same individuals. This is probably a fair representation of most firms operating in the copyright industries, including the music industry (see Karlsson & Lekvall 2002: 11). As the copyright firm evolves, it generates profits that can be accumulated in the firm and used for various future projects. Some larger projects might nevertheless require additional capital, for instance the production of a movie or investment in new studio facilities. In these instances, the smaller copyright firm might turn to a bank to borrow additional capital (Picard 2002: 172), thereby giving it access to capital without having to relinquish control. However, larger copyright firms have for many years turned to the public stock markets to get access to capital.[9] The larger firms require considerable financial resources to support their investments in expensive technologies, expansions into new territories, etc. A publicly traded firm has considerably better access to capital compared with an unlisted firm. In addition, the firm is able to use its own shares as currency, which facilitates mergers with, and acquisitions of, other firms.

Firms listed for trade on a public stock market get access to capital in exchange for ownership of the firm. Although there are many pros in having access to a public stock market, there are also some considerable cons. Investors constantly scrutinize a publicly listed firm, and its financial performance is compared with every other investment opportunity available. Since the deregulation and internationalization of the financial markets during the last two or three decades, these investment opportunities can range from real estate in Moscow to Mexican biotech companies, Scandinavian hedge funds and literally thousands of other objects (Albarran & Chan-Olmsted 1998; Castells 1996; Picard 2002: 185). If the copyright firm is unable to avoid below-average financial performance in comparison to the other options, investors will simply move their monies elsewhere. When this happens, Adam Smith's invisible hand will lower the share price until investors will once again regard the shares as good value for money. This logic puts the publicly traded copyright firm in a situation where the decision regarding what profits are good enough is determined by the international financial market rather than by the management of the firm. The firm has to deliver maximum profits to satisfy the shareholders' quest for highest possible return on investment, otherwise the future of the firm is jeopardized. In other words, when a firm is listed for trade on a public stock market, the only profit good enough is the maximum (Knight 1998; Picard 2002).

A note from the evolutionary economist is required here. Claiming that the firm's goal is profit maximization is not to claim that the firm makes continuous rational decisions that lead to profit maximization. As noted by Cyert and March (1992[1963]), the decision-making process is complex, and often the firm's decisions are not rational and not at all based on correct, unbiased information.

Authenticity and creativity

Is it really possible to create 'authentic art' in organizations where profit maximization is one of the most important goals? Can truly creative processes exist under such circumstances? According to the reasoning of Horkheimer, Adorno and their disciples, the combination is simply impossible (Adorno 1941; Horkheimer & Adorno 1944). To achieve authenticity, culture has to be created by a symbol creator who is independent of any commercial pressure. Those who choose to be associated with the 'majors' – major commercial institutions in the copyright industries – are sell-outs or victims, depending on perspective. Negus comments on this way of understanding the music industry: 'On one side are the heroes – the musicians, producers and performers (the creative artists); opposing them are the villains – the record companies and entertainment corporations (the commercial corrupters and manipulators)' (1996: 46).

The concept of the 'major' deserves some further attention. 'Major' is usually the term employed to represent a large copyright firm with operations in several countries and in control of a well-established distribution machinery. The major is often publicly traded or is part of an entertainment conglomerate. This should be compared with 'independent (companies)' or 'Indies', which are usually the opposite of everything above, and have a stronger focus on the text, the creativity and the art, rather than the business. The work created within the realms of an indie is considered to be less a part of the capitalistic system. Based on the logic of Adorno and others, it is also more 'authentic' than a work created within the walls of a major.

But what is authentic art? Another way of approaching the issue is to focus on creativity rather than trying to distinguish the 'authentic' from the 'fake'. The social psychologist Teresa Amabile has done extensive research on creativity within organizations (e.g., 1996; 1998). When defining creativity, she chooses to focus on the output: 'A product or response will be judged as creative to the extent that (a) it is both a novel and appropriate, useful, correct or valuable response to the task at hand, and (b) the task is heuristic rather than algorithmic' (1996: 35). An important question then is whether the 'tasks' within copyright industries are heuristic or algorithmic.[10] Amabile reflects on this issue: '[A]n artist who followed the algorithm "paint pictures of different sorts of children with large sad eyes, using dark-toned backgrounds" would not be producing creative paintings, even if each painting were unique and technically perfect' (1996: 36). This is exactly what is happening in industrial production of culture according to the reasoning of the Frankfurt School. Symbol creators in the copyright industries follow 'an algorithm' in order to deliver products that fulfil certain criteria and hence are commercially successful in the marketplace (Adorno 1941).

Amabile concludes that individual creativity, to a large extent, is dependent on the person's social environment. She stresses the importance of finding your own, internal motivation and being able to stay independent of demands and reactions from the environment. A symbol creator's primary driver has to be the joy, will or need to create for its own sake, independent of whether the product will be received by good reviews or commercial success. Amabile summarizes her conclusions by stating: 'Intrinsic motivation is conducive to creativity, but extrinsic motivation is detrimental' (1996: 15).

Art and commerce in the music industry
Frith (e.g., 1978; 1983) has argued that there is no conflict between art and commerce, at least not in the music industry. Frith claims that rock music, which sometimes is considered as a musical genre with relatively high levels of authenticity, was not created outside the system of commercial music. Rock music was, rather, created within that system, and is a result of combining creativity and commerce. Building on this analysis, Frith concluded that the relationship between art and commerce should not be described as antagonistic, but as integrated. Negus has challenged Frith by pointing to the actual experiences of audiences and artists: 'If those of us who study popular music are to take seriously the vocabularies of participants . . . then the use of clichés . . . in discussions about the music industry cannot simply be dismissed as artistic conceit or audience *naïveté*' (Negus 1996: 47). One such artist who very explicitly explained his feelings of being trapped within the capitalistic system and of being unable to express his creativity is Prince Rogers Nelson (Mitchell 2005; Orwall 1995; Rosen 1994). Prince (as he is known) performed several times with the word 'slave' written on his forehead as a way of describing his strained relationship with his record label at the time; Warner Bros.[11] If the words of Prince and many other symbol creators are taken seriously, there

apparently is some kind of tension between art and commerce, which contrasts the copyright industries to other industries.

Burnett (1990) and other scholars have shown that creative cultural production normally does not take place in large, mature organizations. Rather, it is the smaller firms ('the indies') that are able to create an environment where creativity is intrinsically motivated. Within the domains of popular music, this is confirmed over and over again, as new genres are developed or picked up by the smaller firm long before any larger firm has discovered the novelty. Apparently, the milieu within smaller firms is able to nourish a greater level of creativity than the milieu within larger firms. It has already been discussed in this text how the larger firm has to be more focused on profit maximization than the smaller firm. In addition, the larger firm requires more complex administration, including strategies, budgets, marketing plans, financial reports, etc. All these structures create a whole range of external demands and restrictions. Where the small firm is driven forward by the joy of independence and the pleasure of creating something new (intrinsic motivation), the larger firm is primarily driven forward by the need to fulfil the next financial plan (extrinsic motivation).

In order to address this problem, many larger music companies have created organizational structures with the intention of establishing an environment within the firm that allows creativity to flourish, despite the fact that external demands remain in place. One such structure is based on 'semi-independent' business units within the larger firms (Burnett 1990). These smaller intra-organizational units are given a considerable amount of freedom in the expectations that the intrinsic motivation will drive the business units forward. Hesmondhalgh points to a similar strategy within the copyright industries when he refers to the 'loose control of symbol creators' within copyright industries, which is motivated by the 'long-standing assumptions about the ethical desirability of creative autonomy, which derive from the romantic conception of symbolic creativity, and traditions of free speech' (2002: 22).

Let us now continue with another question of vital importance in this attempt to understand the music industry as a copyright industry. What approach should be used and what tools are needed in order to explore the dynamics of a copyright industry?

Exploring copyright industry dynamics

Exploring copyright industry dynamics basically means exploring the development of a phenomenon during an extended period of time, rather than at a specific moment. Such a study asks questions such as, what kind of change can be observed? What are the drivers of this change, and how does the change in turn affect other parts of the phenomenon? The unit of analysis is primarily the organization, or, more specifically, the music firm. However, this study is also interested in how change occurs on an individual level, such as how roles and responsibilities within an organization evolve over time. As revealed by the title of this book and this section, I am also interested in how the change at individual and organizational levels interplays with dynamics on an industrial level.

The microenvironment of the copyright firm
One classic model for analysing how the industrial environment influences a firm's ability to grow and survive was suggested by Michael Porter in 1980. The model uses concepts from industrial organization economics to derive five 'forces', which together constitute the microenvironment where a firm is operating.[12] Based on an understanding of this environment, managers are able to make strategic decisions regarding how to manoeuvre their organization in order to create competitive advantage. The five forces are presented and briefly discussed below.

1 *Threat of new entrants – barriers to entry and mobility*   Is it likely that new or existing companies might enter the market with competing products or services? The threat of new entrants may

be determined by several different factors. One might be capital requirements: for instance, the financing needed to establish operations and pay start-up losses (Picard 2002: 72). A second potential factor is product differentiation: for instance, if existing firms already have unique products with great consumer loyalty, a new firm will have difficulty in getting a foothold in the market. A third factor is what is known as switching costs: for instance, if consumers acquire a content library from a supplier using a specific media technology, it will be costly for the consumer to switch to another supplier which uses a different, competing technology. Depending on your perspective and specific situation, this mechanism may be referred to as 'lock-in' and is a well-established strategy in many industries (see, e.g., Hax & Wilde 2001; Shapiro & Varian 1999). Limited access to distribution channels – for instance the limited shelf space available for the display of magazines – is also a factor that determines barriers to entry. A new player might, for instance, be unable to gain access to that shelf space, which will make it difficult to enter the market. Finally, government regulations may be a barrier to entry if, for instance, they restrict access to the frequency spectrum available for terrestrial broadcasting.

2 *Substitutability of products or services*   How great is the risk that buyers replace the current product or service with something else, which satisfies the same need, but in a different way? In the copyright industries, products are normally relatively differentiated and the level of substitutability and competition between them is limited. A cheering U2 fan is not very likely to substitute Bono with another artist without great reluctance. Actors operating in other industries often look with envy at the levels of customer loyalty that can be found within the music industry. However, as with most of the forces in Porter's model, substitutability may vary between different parts of a value chain. The same content may, for instance, be distributed using a number of different media technologies (e.g., VHS, DVD and BitTorrent). Even though the substitutability on content level is

low, the substitutability and level of competition between different distribution technologies may be fierce.

3 & 4   Bargaining power of buyers and suppliers   Are the buyers able to negotiate a lower price, improved quality, etc., or are they restricted to accepting whatever is offered? In consumer-oriented businesses, the bargaining power of buyers is generally low. It is not particularly easy to negotiate a lower ticket price at the box office. The corresponding reasoning can be directed towards suppliers. Are the suppliers strong enough to demand higher prices, better contractual terms, etc., or are they restricted to accepting whatever terms are offered by the players in the industry? There are many different kinds of suppliers to a music firm, but if the focus is set on the artist, the bargaining power depends heavily on the artist's previous success. The new and unknown artist has a bargaining power that is close to zero. If the artist wants to get international and physical distribution, there are few other options than to aim for a contract with one of the majors. The terms of these contracts are usually dictated by the record label and accepted by the artist. At the other end of the spectrum is the megastar who is able to act quite differently. In recent years, there have been several cases in which a record label has signed agreements where the firm has taken a large portion of the business risk and a minor portion of the expected profit (e.g., EMI 2002).

5   Rivalry among firms already operating in the market   How intense is the competition between existing actors in the industry? The competition between firms is to a great extent linked to the structure of the industry. Neoclassical economic theory defines a market-structure continuum ranging from monopoly to oligopoly, monopolistic competition and finally to perfect competition (see Hoskins & McFadyen 2004; Wildman 2006: 72–5). Perfect competition is the condition in which a considerable number of similar-sized firms compete with identical products. Consumers are also numerous and have complete and correct information regarding the products and prices offered by the firms competing on the market. Under these conditions, price is usually the only competitive weapon. However, this theoretical condition is not very relevant to the copyright industries: 'Markets for information will not, and cannot, look like textbook-perfect competitive markets in which there are many suppliers offering similar products, each lacking the ability to influence prices' (Shapiro & Varian 1999: 23). Monopolistic competition is somewhat more realistic than perfect competition, since the products offered are differentiated rather than identical. In this kind of market, it is possible to compete by using product innovation, rather than just price. An oligopolistic industry is dominated by a few large firms producing differentiated products. Under these conditions the barriers to entry are usually substantial. The competition between these large players is consequently lower than in the previous two cases. Copyright industries such as music, movie and broadcasting are best described as oligopolies (Hoskins & McFadyen 2004; Picard 2002). Finally, a monopoly is an industry with a single player, and consequently no rivalry at all.

An evolutionary theory of the firm
The five-forces model may be useful when decision-makers carve out a strategy for their business. Early strategy scholars (e.g., Ansoff 1965; Bain 1959) often understood a firm's 'strategy' as a formalized set of rules for making decisions. These decision rules can also be seen as a position that is to be assumed based on where the organization is today and where it wants to be within a certain period of time. Several scholars have followed this school of thought. For instance, Porter (1980) explained strategy as the firm's position taken after the investigation of the competitive environment. According to Porter, there are basically only two ways a firm can compete: either by focusing on low cost or by focusing on product differentiation. It is not possible to successfully combine the two options.

A different way of thinking about strategy was suggested by

Wernerfelt. While Porter emphasizes external factors, Wernerfelt (1984) argues that the basis for a firm's competitive advantage primarily lies in its ability to develop, sustain and apply a bundle of valuable resources. Resources should in this context be understood as the firm's assets, capabilities, routines, processes, skills, knowledge, etc. (see also Barney 1991).

During the 1990s, strategy scholars added to this body of research by recognizing the increasing volatility and uncertainty in many industries. This turned the focus of organizational theorists from questions regarding which strategic position is most appropriate during a specific environmental condition, to a firm's ability to assume new strategic positions as swiftly as possible. Competition is not as much a 'war of position' as it is a 'war of movement' (Ghemawat 1991; Hamel & Prahalad 1993; Porter 1991; Stalk 1988; Stalk et al. 1992; Sterman 1994).

Building on Wernerfelt's resource-based view, the concept of 'movements' translates into a question of how a firm is able continuously to revise and develop its resources and capabilities in order to adapt to a volatile and uncertain environment. When applied to the music industrial context, this question lies at the core of this book, since it examines how digital technologies affect the production, promotion, distribution and consumption of music and how the music business is being fundamentally transformed in order to survive in a digital age.

Previous research into this field has to a large extent been based on the works by Nelson and Winter (1982) on organizational routines, Cohen and Levinthal (1990) on absorptive capacity, Teece et al. (1997) on dynamic capabilities and Argyris & Schön (1978) on organizational learning, or on some other similar framework. What is common to all these frameworks is that they rest on other basic microeconomic assumptions than many older theories, including Porter's five-forces model. The frameworks all rely on evolutionary economic theory rather than on neoclassical economic theory. Since evolutionary economics is fundamental to the perspective I am using in this book, I shall look into what differentiates this theory from its ancestors and relatives.

Evolutionary concepts in economic theory started to emerge at the beginning of the twentieth century as an answer to a growing discomfort with the established neoclassical economic models. There are several problems with neoclassical economic models, which, according to evolutionary economists, make them 'barren and irrelevant as an apparatus of thought' (Kaldor 1972: 1237). One is that they focus heavily on equilibrium, optimum and static structures and do not actually describe the complex dynamics of an economy. If change occurs in neoclassical economic models, it occurs only within the given and static structures. In addition, neoclassical economics is generally based on the assumption that organizations and individuals make well-informed, rational decisions in order to maximize their financial wealth.

Evolutionary economists argue that the assumptions of neoclassical economic theory make it difficult to explain actual economic behaviour. Societal and economic systems are often not in equilibrium, and socioeconomic structures do change, sometimes quite dramatically. Also, individuals and organizations are often unable to make well-informed decisions, and, frequently, these decisions are biased and irrational, contrary to neoclassical economic theory (see, e.g., England 1994; Simon 1979).

Evolutionary economics is often linked to Darwin's publication of *On the Origin of Species* in 1859. Darwinian change differs from non-evolutionary Newtonian change in that the first is caused by changes in system structure, while the latter represents change within a given structure (Hamilton 1953). The distinction can be used to differentiate economic growth (more of the same) from economic development (structural change) (Boulding 1981). During the twentieth century, several scholars continued to mould the framework of evolutionary economics. Many aspects of Joseph Schumpeter's reasoning are evolutionary in their character. His model of innovation and economic change is probably the most apparent example (1911), but his tendency towards evolutionary economics is also apparent in his discussions regarding Marxist economic theory: 'The essential point is that in dealing with capitalism we are dealing with an evolutionary process. It may seem strange that anyone can fail to see so obvious a fact which moreover was long ago emphasized by Karl Marx' (Schumpeter 1942: 82). Other scholars (e.g., Nelson & Winter 1982; Radzicki & Sterman 1994) have continued to contribute to the field by adding other metaphors and concepts to the framework. Myrdal (1956) introduced the theory of circular and cumulative causation and Boulding (e.g., 1968; 1978; 1981) applied the second law of thermodynamics and the concepts of time irreversibility to the analysis of economic systems. Others contributed with theories of self-organization, complexity and chaos to explain organizations' adaptive processes (e.g., Foster & Metcalfe 2001; Lorenz 1989; Radzicki 1990; Varian 1979; Witt 2003).

Further, March and Simon (1958) and Cyert and March (1992[1963]) used an evolutionary approach when they developed the behavioural theory of the firm. They explained intra-organizational decision-making by using the concept of bounded rationality – that is, the fact that decision-makers are not well informed and rational, but sometimes pretty far from that description. This understanding of organizational decision-making can be traced further to the models of organizational learning presented, for instance, by Argyris and Schön (1978) and later by Senge (1990).

The process of organizational adaptation

Like many other organizational theorists working in the spirit of evolutionary economic theory, Miles and Snow (1978) observed that different organizations react differently to environmental change. They suggested a simple typology consisting of four types of organization (defenders, prospectors, analysers and reactors), each with its own way of adapting to environmental change (1978: 30).

Defenders are organizations producing a limited set of products directed at a narrow segment of the market. Their most important strategic question is how to produce and distribute goods and services as efficiently as possible. The management team of the defender is usually dominated by production and cost-control specialists and has little or no expertise focused on scanning the environment for new product or market opportunities. Since these firms have chosen this organizational structure, their greatest risk is that of being unable to respond to a major shift in their environment. Consequently, the defender strategy and structure is most viable in stable industries, such as mining or food-processing (Miles & Snow 1978; Miles et al. 1978).

Prospectors are organizations that in many respects are the opposite of the defenders. Their prime capability is that of finding and exploiting new product and market opportunities. The prospectors' domain of markets and products is usually broad and in a continuous state of development. They are frequently the creators of change in their industries, and change and innovation are often their major tools in gaining an edge over their competitors. For prospectors, the reputation as an innovator is as important as, perhaps even more important than, high profitability. In fact, because of this prioritization and the inevitable 'failure rate' associated with sustained product and market innovation, prospectors may find it difficult to consistently reach the profit levels of the more efficient defenders (Miles & Snow 1978).

While defenders and prospectors reside at opposite ends of a continuum of adaptation strategies, the analyser – the third type – is the balanced combination of the two extremes. A true analyser is an organization that attempts to minimize risk while maximizing the opportunity for profit. To achieve this aim, analysers usually operate in several product-market domains, some relatively stable, others changing. In their stable areas, these organizations operate routinely and efficiently through use of formalized structures and processes. In their more turbulent areas, top managers watch their competitors closely for new ideas, and then rapidly adopt those ideas that appear to be the most promising (Miles & Snow 1978).

Miles and Snow's fourth type, the reactor, is not really an adaptation strategy, but rather the lack thereof. An organization of this type acts inconsistently and seldom makes adjustments of any sort until it is absolutely forced to do so by environmental pressures. Unless the organization is operating in a monopolistic or highly regulated industry, it cannot continue to behave as a reactor indefinitely. Sooner or later, it must move towards one of the consistent and stable strategies of defender, analyser or prospector.

Previously, I have recognized that the music industry is both a volatile and chaotic environment. Based on that observation and combined with the reasoning of Miles and Snow, one might argue that in the music industry, the 'prospector-like' firm has a much greater sustainability than the 'defender-like' firm.

Communities of practice

Evolutionary economic theory generally has a firm- or industry-level focus on dynamic processes and is very useful when exploring how music firms have evolved together with the industry in which they operate. However, changes in the music industry also take place on an individual level, in addition to those on the firm or industry level. One way to understand these processes is to turn to the Communities of Practice (CoP) framework, which originates from the work of Lave and Wenger (1991), and has been brought to the mainstream of organizational theory by Brown and Duguid (1991).

Although they have different intellectual heritages – economics and social learning theories – evolutionary economics and CoP have been applied to investigate somewhat similar organizational phenomena.

Wenger defines a CoP as a 'group of people who share a concern or a passion for something they do and learn how to do it better as they interact regularly' (Wenger 2006). Wenger also notes that not all communities are a CoP, and that, in order to be described as such, three characteristics have to be fulfilled:

(1) *A domain.* Members of a CoP do not necessarily have to know each other but they have to share an interest and

passion in a certain domain. The domain can, for instance, be based on a certain musical instrument or genre.

(2) *A community.* The members must engage in activities that allow them to learn from each other. Various kinds of media can support such activities – for example, magazines or websites. However, it is important to note that an online community in itself does not automatically qualify as a CoP.

(3) *A practice.* A CoP is indeed a community of practitioners and not a community of interest. It is not enough to have a shared interest; the members of a CoP develop certain skills, experiences and tools, which they actively use in their practice.

The CoP framework tries to explain how norms, values, beliefs and routines evolve. How does an individual learn what is the right way of doing things, what it actually means to be a music producer, etc.? How does collective knowledge develop within a CoP? According to this framework, these norms and structures are continuously constructed through a learning process in which individual 'learners do not receive or even construct abstract, "objective", individual knowledge; rather they learn to function in a community . . . They acquire that particular community's subjective viewpoint and learn to speak its language. In short, they are "enculturated"' (Brown et al. 1989).

Production of culture
The frameworks and theories discussed so far have a heritage in economic and organizational theory and treat the copyright industries as an economic activity like most other economic activities. These frameworks are certainly potent tools for analysing the new music economy. However, it is also important to enrich the theoretical toolbox with frameworks that consider music, movies, videogames, books, etc. as, first and foremost, cultural artefacts which, in various ways, interact with society and, second, commodities aimed for trade and consumption.

One theoretical lens with such an emphasis is literary studies, or its relatives: musicology, film studies, cultural studies, etc. However, although literary and cultural studies may be useful frameworks when exploring culture, I have not involved them in this book, since they do not focus on musical products per se. This book is primarily focused on how and why these products are produced, which makes it more relevant to add selected aspects of the vast field of sociology of culture into the theoretical toolbox.

The study of popular culture within the field of sociology can be traced back to the first half of the last century (e.g., Adorno 1941; Weber 1921), but it has only been considered as a serious topic since the 1970s (Dowd 2002; Hirsch & Fiss 2000; Peterson 2000). Earlier, 'mass culture' could perhaps be studied as a social problem, but the 'culture industry' was not considered to be a relevant topic for research. During the 1970s, a young breed of sociologists began to approach culture and the organizations in which culture is produced. These researchers tried to 'depoliticize' the topic by treating it less as a social concern and more as just another challenge for economic and organizational analysts (Hirsch & Fiss 2000).

One of these sociologists, Richard Peterson, charted new ground in an article 'Cycles in Symbol Production: The Case of Popular Music', published with David Berger in *American Sociological Review* in 1975. In this article, Peterson and Berger explored copyright industry dynamics by linking the level of industry concentration within the music industry to the diversity of cultural output. Based on their empirical material, covering 26 years, they were able to conclude that a high level of concentration causes a low level of diversity and vice versa. Hirsch and Fiss (2000) recognize the importance of that article.

It opened the door to enable sociologists to analyse the popular arts descriptively and non-pejoratively, leaving the normative and critical aspects to other fields. In keeping with the discipline's focus of that time, here was a connection to social structure and markets that was no longer critical of the capitalistic framework, thereby enabling the field to approach aesthetics without judging the quality. In fact, the content or quality of the product is irrelevant, or simply a 'matter of taste' that remains external to the framework. Whether leisure time is spent at wrestling matches or opera or baseball is immaterial (Hirsch & Fiss 2000: 100).

Building on the seminal article, Peterson (e.g., 1976; 1979; 1982; 1985) developed the 'production of culture' perspective, which has since become a significant part of production-related research within the sociology of culture. Peterson challenged the notion that cultural products are 'the work of individual artists from whom they are then filtered to the public' (Negus 1997: 99). Instead, Peterson argued that 'the nature and content of symbolic products, are shaped by the social, legal and economic milieu in which they are produced' (1982: 143).

To be able to analyse these milieus, Peterson suggested a set of facets 'which alone, or in combination, often constrain or facilitate the evolution of culture' (1982: 143). The number of facets proposed by Peterson varies between different texts. In one text (1982), Peterson gives a brief presentation of his perspective and considers five facets to constrain or facilitate the production of popular culture: technology, law, organizational structure, occupational careers and market. In another text (1985), where Peterson analyses the publishing industry, a sixth facet, industry structure, has been added to the previous five. Peterson's understanding of these six facets is briefly discussed below and illuminated by examples taken from the copyright industries.

Technology   Technology is used in most kinds of cultural production. If technology changes in some way or another, it will have an implication for the texts being produced. It is easy to identify cases in the history of music production where technology has changed the sound of recorded music: musical instruments – for instance, the piano, the electric guitar or the sampler; recording technologies – for instance, sophisticated microphones, multichannel recording or, more recently, nonlinear recording; distribution technologies – for instance, the vinyl disk, the compact cassette, the compact disk or the Internet (see, e.g., Coleman 2003).

Law 'Statute law and government regulation shape the financial and aesthetic conditions within which popular culture develops' (Peterson 1982: 144). The very term 'copyright' is a legal term, and it is copyright law that transforms cultural expressions into goods that can be traded, bought, sold or infringed.

Industry structure '[T]he number and relative sizes of the firms in the market producing aesthetic products' (Peterson 1982:144). This facet was indirectly in line with the 1975 Peterson and Berger article, where they established a relationship between industry structure and cultural diversity.

Organizational structure This refers to the structures within the boundaries of the firm, coordinating the activities that generate the cultural products. Sometimes organizational structure and industry structure overlap, for instance as a result of the development of 'network organizations' (Castells 1996) where the actual boundary of a firm may be difficult to determine.

Occupational careers '[T]he ways that creative people define their occupations and organize their careers can influence the nature of the work they produce' (Peterson 1982: 148). This facet can be illustrated by how the role of the studio engineer has developed parallel to the development of studio recording technologies. In the beginning of the history of recorded music, the studio engineer was very much someone skilled at handling the equipment in the studio, making sure that the artist's creative ideas were transferred to record in as undistorted a way as possible. Nowadays, the studio engineer is considered to be a musician and sometimes even a star, just like other musicians participating in the recording session (Kealy 1982; Levine & Werde 2003).

Table 1.1 Levels of aggregation and the facets of the production of culture perspective	
Level of aggregation	*Related facets*
Individual	Occupational career
Organization	Organizational structure
Industry	Market
	Technology
	Law
	Industry structure

Market   The final facet, termed 'market', is a reference to the audience, and specifically to how 'financial decision makers redefine the heterogeneous and unknown mass of potential consumers into a homogeneous and predicable "market" that can be tapped through standard market practices' (Peterson 1982:146).

The production of culture perspective is significantly different from the economic and organizational theories previously discussed, not only in terms of its emphasis on cultural products as artefacts rather than commodities, but also in its very structure. The production of culture perspective is able to cover all three levels that interest me in this study: individual, organizational and industrial (see Table 1.1).

Industry dynamics research initiatives typically start with the observation of some kind of change. The change may involve new products or genres, changes in consumer behaviour, technology changes, regulatory changes, change in aggregate sales, change in financial performance, change in organizational or industry structures, change in (production/distribution/marketing) routines, etc. The purpose of such a research initiative is then to gain more knowledge about this change, possibly to be able to understand or explain why the change has occurred or how it might influence some aspect of the industry. However, the complexity of economic and social systems often makes such attempts very difficult, sometimes even impossible. This is noted by Peterson, who considers his production perspective to be a 'retreat from confronting the unanswerable questions about the causal links between society and culture' (1994: 185). Miles and Snow have also reflected on the difficulty of examining these dynamic processes: 'Any attempt to examine organizational adaptation is difficult since the process is both highly complex and changeable' (1978: 4).

It is consequently important to have the right equipment when engaging in such an apparently arduous exercise. I have gathered my theoretical lenses from the fields of organizational theory, social learning theory and sociology of culture. The frameworks have various intellectual traditions, they complement each other and they share several fundamental qualities. By using these frameworks in concert, we are now ready to explore the dynamics of the music industry in the digital age.

2

Inside the Music Industry

While the previous chapter focused on copyright industries in general, this chapter will take a look inside the music industry. It introduces and discusses various definitions of the music industry and it tries to locate its boundaries. Three segments of the industry are identified – music-recording, music-licensing and live music – and a number of fundamental characteristics for each sub-industry are presented. This is then followed by a brief look in the rear-view mirror, tracing the evolution of the industry during the last century. The chapter will also present some facts and figures of the world's six largest multinational music firms.

What do I mean by the 'music industry'?

An industry is traditionally considered to be a specific part of the economy concerned with the factory production of goods aimed for mass consumption. Since the beginning of the industrial revolution, the concept of an 'industry' has expanded beyond that traditional definition and is now generally used to refer to the production, marketing and distribution of most commodities, including services and immaterial goods. There are several ways to classify and structure different industrial activities. One of the more common ways is to refer to primary, secondary and tertiary industries; the first category includes, for example, mining and agriculture; the second category includes primarily manufacturing industries; and the third category is concerned with service production. Other ways of structuring industries are, for instance, light versus heavy industries, business-to-business versus business-to-consumer industries, etc. However,

Table 2.1   The music industry as defined by the British government

Core activities	Supporting activities	Related industries
Production, distribution and retailing of sound recordings	Music press	Internet/e-commerce
	Multimedia content	Television and radio
Administration of copyright in composition and recordings	Digital media	Film and video
	Retailing and distribution of digital music via the Internet	Advertising
Live performance (non-classical)		Performance arts
	Music for computer games	Interactive leisure software
Management, representation and promotion	Art and creative studios	Software and computer services
Song-writing and composition	Production, distribution and retailing of printed music	
	Production, retailing and distribution of musical instruments	
	Jingle production	
	Photography	
	Education and training	

Source: DCMS 1998

perhaps the most common way to define an industry is to refer to the output from the industrial activity – for instance, the travel, automotive or consumer electronics industry. Within any such industry it is also common to structure activities as core, supporting or related.

Several attempts have been made to define and structure the different parts of the music industry. One such attempt has been presented by the UK government's Department for Culture, Media and Sport, which over the years has presented a number of reports on the state of the UK music industry (DCMS 1998). Another quite useful definition has been suggested by Engström and Hallencreutz (2003). Tables 2.1 and 2.2 show that there are some differences between the two definitions. It is of course important to policymakers, trade organizations and others to define the scope and reach of 'their' industries. However, since

Table 2.2 The music industry according to Engström and Hallencreutz	
Music industry organizations	*Related industries*
Music press	Daily press
Record labels/producers/studios	Other retailers, e.g. gas stations
Music publishers	Hotels
Mastering studios	Restaurants, pubs, clubs
Suppliers of stage equipment	Catering
Distributors and wholesalers	Photography
Music retailers	Graphic design
Retailers of music instruments and studio equipment	Video production
E-business	Broadcasting
Management	Stylists
Artists/musicians/performers	Lawyers and auditors
Tour production and concert arrangements	
Artist agencies	

Source: Engström and Hallencreutz 2003: 39

most copyright industries are evolving, lists such as the ones presented in these tables usually become out-dated relatively quickly.

Negus (1992) approaches the definition issue from a different perspective. He describes the music industry as 'concerned with developing global personalities which can be communicated across multiple media: through recordings, videos, films, television, magazines, books and via advertising, product endorsement and sponsorship over a range of consumer merchandise' (1992: 1). In this book, I choose to improve upon Negus's definition, by suggesting two minor adjustments. First, I remove the word 'global' since there are many musical artists that are simply not intended for a global market. Second, I add the words 'musical content', to emphasize the importance of controlling and developing different kinds of intellectual properties. These changes

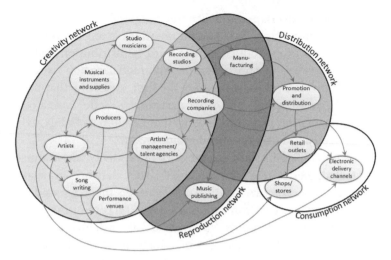

Source: Leyshon 2001

Figure 2.1   Musical networks

result in the following music industry definition, which I will use throughout this book: 'The music industry consists of those companies concerned with developing musical content and personalities which can be communicated across multiple media.'

Three integrated music industries

When trying to stay above the nitty-gritty details of what is or is not part of the music industry, one can generally consider it to be made up of three parts: recording, publishing and live performance (Hesmondhalgh 2002: 12). Several scholars have tried to explain the logic and dynamics of all these areas, often by presenting various kinds of conceptual industry models.

Leyshon suggests one such model (see Figure 2.1), which emphasizes that 'the music economy consists of a series of sequential processes' (2001: 57). Building on this understanding, Leyshon's model is primarily based on Attali (1985) and Scott (1999) and constitutes four 'musical networks' which 'possess distinctive but overlapping functions, temporalities, and geographies' (Leyshon 2001: 60). The first network is one of creativity, the second is of reproduction, the third is distribution and the last is a network of consumption. Although Leyshon uses the terms 'network', it is actually only the first, creativity, that has a network-like structure. The other parts of the model have a relatively linear structure, which means that Leyshon's model can be categorized as a fairly traditional value chain.

The model begins with the network of creativity where music is created, performed and recorded. This network gravitates around the contractual relationship between the artist and the record company. Leyshon explains this as the core of the music industry, where elements such as artists, producers, studio musicians, sound engineers, music instruments and supplies, song-writing, artist management, legal services, performance venues, recording studios and recording companies are found (Leyshon 2001).

Beyond the network of creativity, the networks of reproduction, distribution and consumption are primarily focused on recording and pay less attention to the two other industry sectors.

Being a geographer, Leyshon puts lots of emphasis on the spatial issues of the music industry. Consequently, in the networks termed 'distribution' and 'consumption', where he includes physical promotion, distribution, retail stores and consumers, he is more interested in how the CDs are moved from one place to another than how the music firms are able to raise the consumer's awareness of a certain project. This stands in stark contrast to, for instance, the model introduced by Hirsch (presented later in this chapter) which is focused on the promotion and marketing of music rather than on how the physical product is transported from the manufacturing site to the consumers.

Another model, which also aims to explain the dynamics of the music industries, is the 'loosely coupled systems model' suggested by Burnett and Weber (1989; see figure 2.2). 'Loosely coupled' refers to systems in which interactions within subsystems are substantially stronger than interactions between

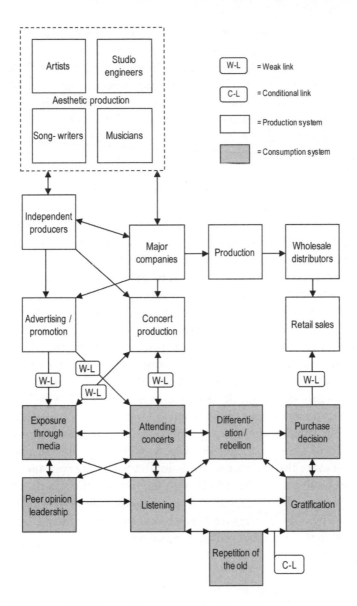

Source: Burnett & Weber 1989

Figure 2.2   Production/consumption systems of popular music

sub-systems (see, for example, Brunner & Brewer 1971; Fisher 1961; Glassman 1973; March & Olsen 1976; Meyer & Rowan 1978; Ouchi 1978; Perrow 1986; Simon 1981; Simon & Ando 1961; Weick 1976). The Burnett and Weber model consists of more or less the same components as Leyshon's model, but the structure is somewhat different. The model is not a linear structure describing how consumer value is created; rather, it shows how different activities or institutions in the industry are related (Burnett & Weber 1989).

This model is structured as two loosely connected systems of production and of consumption. The production system is distinct from the consumption system meaning that the connections and ties within these systems are substantially stronger than the connections and ties between them. The relations among record producers, artists, marketing and promotion specialists, trade press and so on are stronger than the relationships between producers and consumers. Consumers of music, on the other hand, interact among themselves, today increasingly via social media. The mainly separate systems of production and consumption are connected through the media, concerts and also an economic act: the purchase of music. In the model, the aggregate behaviour of each system is such that it weakly influences the behaviour of the other.

The musical networks model (Leyshon 2001) and the loosely coupled systems model (Burnett & Weber 1989) both point at aspects of the traditional music industry that are common to all three sub-sectors. Next I will shift the focus to the specific music industry sub-sectors and examine their distinguishing features, starting out with the sector which dominated the music industry during the twentieth century: music-recording.

Recording
The record company's traditional business model involves the production of intellectual properties by recording artists' studio or live performances. The record company then markets and distributes these recordings to consumers around the world.

The sociologist Paul Hirsch was one of the first to analyse the recording industry in a serious manner. In 1970 he presented a model with the purpose of explaining how music becomes popular. Hirsch's model describes the sector of the recording industry that is traditionally referred to as the 'top 40 music industry'. The 'top 40' format was invented in the US during the 1950s when the new medium of television forced the radio medium to change its programming (see, e.g., Thorburn & Jenkins 2003). A radio station that adhered to this particular format played the 40 most popular songs during a certain week. 'Most popular' was in this case equal to the records that had sold the most during the previous week. Even to this day, most commercial mainstream radio stations follow a similar format. 'Top 40' is today referred to as 'contemporary hit radio' (CHR) and is but one of many different radio formats. Other formats include classic rock, country, urban, adult contemporary (AC), news/talk, oldies, modern rock, classical and smooth jazz.

The record labels producing music aimed for the 'top 40 music industry' are heavily dependent on the commercial radio stations for the promotion of their artists and music. Hirsch recognized the close relationship between the two copyright industries: 'The record and radio industry have grown up together and live in a symbiotic relationship. Each plays an important role in the dissemination and popularization of culture; both have affected its form and its direction. Although mutually dependent organizations, their goals vary, and oftimes conflict' (1970: 10). This relationship is clearly illustrated in Figure 2.3, where the 'pop music industry' is mapped to the preselection system framework.[13]

A large amount of 'filtering' takes place at each of the stages of the preselection system. Only a small fraction of all artists are ever able even to meet an A&R (artist and repertoire) agent, and only very few out of all the acts that an A&R agent ever listens to attract the attention of the record executive. Eventually, only one artist 'in a million' will be heard by the mainstream audience on commercial radio stations.

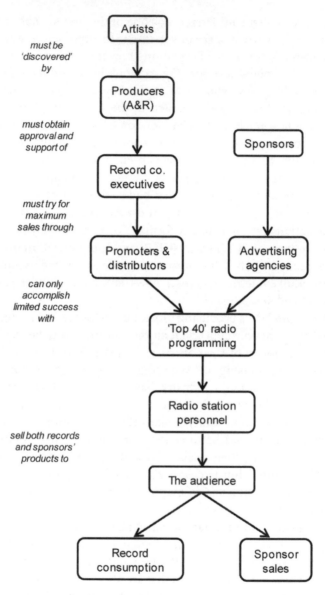

Source: Hirsch 1970:17A

Figure 2.3   The organization of the recording industry

Hirsch has identified four sub-systems within the music industry that the artist has to pass through to be able to reach the final sub-system: the audience. Below, Hirsch's understanding of these four sub-systems will be briefly presented.

The first sub-system is the creative sector, including the artist, the producer and the A&R agent. Hirsch states that 'the success of every performing artist is closely tied to the number of his records that come to the attention of and are purchased by the public. Records are the means by which an artist gains or enlarges his popular following' (1970: 25). The A&R agent is the first strategic checkpoint in the preselection process that eventually may take the artist all the way to commercial success. The agents have a crucial job since they are the ones who will find new talents with artistic as well as commercial potential. It is critical to each record company to continuously find new talents, since the life of a 'hit' record lasts only 60–120 days. 'Replacements are needed for those items currently on the "charts". The unknown artist and the companies each share a vital interest in his discovery and success, for the hit record industry is based on the fads of the moment. The styles in vogue change rapidly and unpredictably' (Hirsch 1970: 25).

The second sub-system is the record company. When an artist has been discovered by an A&R agent, the next step is to meet the record company policymakers. These men and women have the task of selecting from the output of the creative sub-system the records that are to be released (Hirsch 1970: 31). Hirsch notes that 'while the decision to release a record is theirs, policymakers have little control over the media, little power to ensure the exposure of a particular release. Record companies' promotion of some artists at the expense of others (all under contract to them) is in large part an attempt to structure the ambiguity of this situation' (1970: 33).

Promoters and distributors constitute the third sub-system. The function of this sub-system is to filter the output from policymakers at the record companies. In the scenario described by Hirsch, there are far more record companies than there are promoters. In such a situation, the promoters add value to the process by selecting the songs that they expect to have the best chance of commercial success.

The final sub-system is labelled 'gatekeepers' and is constituted by radio stations and other media outlets. The interdependence between gatekeepers and record companies has already been mentioned. Hirsch adds to the description of this symbiotic relationship by claiming that 'radio airplay for a new record is almost always a prerequisite for its sale' (Hirsch 1970: 9).[14] However, only very few out of all the albums released are able to get into gatekeepers' playlists. Hirsch continues:

> Radio station managements demand high audience ratings, for the rates charged to advertising sponsors (i.e. the station's income) are based solely on the number of listeners the station can 'deliver'. Advertising agencies place ads with radio stations according to the 'cost per thousand' listeners. The fierce competition between stations requires that the program director successfully select a group of records that will appeal to the widest possible audience. (Hirsch 1970: 61)

Consequently, 'the record promoter . . . must operate within the context of the station programmer's quest for certainty. The programme director is constantly on the lookout for advance intelligence regarding the "hit" potential of every record he selects for airplay' (Hirsch 1970: 56). The record promoter tries to address this request by providing sales figures to demonstrate his records' popularity.

Hirsch's model was the fruition of one of the first attempts to explore the music industry. A reasonable question is whether the model has any relevance nearly half a century after it was developed. Through the years, the model has certainly been criticized, but it still is able to encapsulate important aspects of the workings of the mainstream recording industry. For instance, there are still gatekeepers in the new music economy even though they look very different from those of the 1970s. Music still has to be exposed to the audience in order for listeners to be able to determine its value. Broadcast radio is to some extent losing its importance, but is still an important component in music promotion. Advertisers or sponsors are probably even more important to the music industry today than they were 50 years ago.

Publishing

While the recording industry is a business-to-consumer industry, the music publishing segment of the music industry nowadays has almost no direct contact with the music audience. Composers and lyricists engage a publisher to license their works for various purposes, such as traditional recordings, sheet music, live performances or background music in video productions. The royalties paid by the licensee flow via various mechanisms to the composer or lyricist as one of three different royalty categories. Performance royalties are paid when a song is performed by an orchestra or singer, played by a radio station, used as a mobile phone ringtone, played in a shopping mall, etc. Synchronization royalties are paid when a song is used together with moving images, for instance a movie or a videogame. Mechanical royalties are paid based on actual sales of sheet music and audio recordings (see Vogel 2001: 157–8). Traditionally, music publishing royalties are split 50/50, with half going to the publisher as payment for their services and the rest going to the composers and lyricists.

CISAC (2012), the International Confederation of Societies of Authors and Composers, reported that, in 2010, the global value of music-related royalties was approximately $8.7 billion (€6.5 billion). CISAC is a confederation of regional and national organizations (so-called 'royalty collection societies') that collect royalties from music users (radio stations, restaurants, etc.) and distribute them to rights holders. It should be noted that the CISAC estimate only includes royalties reported by its members; even though it includes most of the world's music publishing royalties, it does not, for instance, include royalties paid directly by the licensee to the owner of the property that are not administered by a royalty collection society.

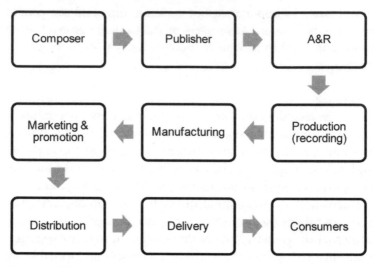

Source: Wallis 2004:105

Figure 2.4   A music publishing industry value chain

Figure 2.4 shows a music industry value chain, with a specific focus on music publishing and the licensing of songs to record companies. The model explains how the composer creates the work and normally signs an agreement with a publisher. In Wallis's value chain, the only possibility is to have the song picked up by a record company's A&R department and subsequently recorded by an artist. There are of course other opportunities and revenue sources available to the composer. These are recognized by Wallis, but left out of the graphical representation.

Live performance
The recorded music sector has historically been bigger than the live music sector in terms of revenues, but during recent years revenues from live music seem to have overtaken recorded music as the largest music industry sector (Laing 2012; Page 2011).

The live music segment of the music industry is a multifaceted and complex system. Live music is performed in busy streets and subway stations, at private parties and rock festivals, in local pubs, clubs, sports arenas and amphitheatres. The concerts can be one-off shows, tours or a series of shows at a single venue. These characteristics of the industry make it very difficult to measure and analyse. It is difficult to delineate the industry and to gather data, for instance, for all the smaller gigs played at pubs and private parties around the world. Most of the attention is, for obvious reasons, given to the largest and most spectacular global tours with the brightest shining superstars. However, this part of the industry is interesting not just because of its glamour; the live music industry is very top-heavy in the sense that a small number of big projects constitute a large percentage of the total industry. The 'top-heaviness' of the industry adds to the measurement difficulties, as the size of the industry varies greatly between different years depending on which artists decide to go on tour that particular year. In spite of these difficulties, several reports have estimated that the total value of the global live music sector during 2011 was in the range of $20–25 billion (see, e.g., Laing 2012; eMarketer 2012).

There are four important actors operating in the live music industry: obviously the performers, but there are also the booking agents, the promoters and the venue operators. The booking agent works on behalf of the artist and contracts the promoter to arrange the events. Booking agents usually get a fixed fee or a percentage fee from the performer, and the promoters earn their revenue primarily from the sales of tickets. The performers are paid by the promoters according to a formula that may differ between artists and between events. The formula usually includes a guaranteed payment and a percentage of ticket sales or event revenues. The performers may be reimbursed for various production costs such as sound or lights. Promoters, together with the performers, managers and booking agents, jointly determine the price of the tickets, an important issue to which I will return later in this section. The promoters normally market the events, sell tickets, make agreements with local venue operators, etc. The venue operators normally provide additional services such as parking, security, ticket-collecting, etc. The venue operators typically receive percentages of the ticket sales as well as of concession sales and merchandise sales.

The North American and the European live music sectors are currently both dominated by Live Nation Entertainment. Since a few years back, the publicly listed company has been the world's largest music company. It is even larger than Universal Music Group, which before the downturn of the recorded music business was the longstanding subscriber of the position as industry leader. Live Nation's dominant position has been criticized by competitors, consumer organizations and touring artists. In some regional markets, Live Nation owns or controls every single music venue of significance, which means that it efficiently governs which artists are allowed to perform in that market. In a similar fashion, the company, through the 2010 acquisition of the ticketing sales company Ticketmaster, controls a majority of the ticket sales business in a number or geographical music markets, most notably the United States. The company's dominance of the global live music sector is not equally strong, but Live Nation nevertheless controls about 25 per cent of that market. It should be noted, however, that this value varies between different geographical markets and different stages in the value chain.

Although considerably outdistanced by Live Nation, the second largest actor in the live music industry is AEG Live, a subsidiary of Anschutz Entertainment Group. AEG Live has expanded its live music business and has established itself as the global number two. Beyond these two multinationals, the global live music industry is very fragmented and primarily consists of national or regional players.

A brief history of the music-recording industry

In order to understand the contemporary music-recording industry, it is important to know where the industry is coming from. The history of music may be traced back to the Upper

Palaeolithic age, and sometimes even further back, but the historical account in this section will have a somewhat shorter scope. The historical narrative will follow the evolution of the industrial aspects of music culture, and especially those aspects that are related to music-recording. There are several accounts of the history of the international recording industry (e.g., Barfe 2004; Coleman 2003; Gelatt 1977; Gronow 1983; Gronow & Saunio 1998; Qualen 1985; Read & Welch 1976). This section is primarily based on these sources.

The history of the music-recording industry can be described in many ways. One is to focus on how different genres have evolved and been rejected or embraced by the business and the audience. Another is to use technological milestones as the framework for laying out the industry's evolution and to follow how formats for distribution, listening devices or production technologies and musical instruments have developed. This is the perspective I will start out with in this account, but I will also try to combine the technological perspective with a focus on the major firms of the recording industry. Primarily, I will focus on how firms have been established and discontinued, and how firms have acquired or merged with each other.

Music has been the basis of viable businesses for centuries, but, through the ages, the balance between the three segments of recording, publishing and live performance has fluctuated. Before the advent of print technology, the music industry consisted of only one of the three segments, namely the live per-formance business. Obviously, it is somewhat anachronistic to ascribe terms such as 'industry' to the work of musicians of this age. The activities of musicians outside the churches, monaster-ies and royal courts were not very industrial in character, but at least the musicians were able to make a living through their trade. As print technology evolved, sheet music slowly became a second product that could be sold to the growing European urban middle classes. At the end of the nineteenth century and beginning of the twentieth, those who wanted to listen to music most likely had to play it themselves. They learned about music from friends or by listening to performers at local bandstands and vaudevilles. When they heard a song that they liked, those who could afford it bought the sheet music at the local stationery store and played the popular piece on the piano in their living room. One of the most successful works during the turn of the twentieth century was 'After the Ball', by Charles Harris, which was popularized at the Chicago World's Fair, and sold more than two million sheet-music copies. In 1907, another song, 'School Days' by Gus Edwards, sold more than three million copies.

The centre of gravity in the industry producing the sheet music was located in New York City, on 28th Street between Broadway and Sixth Avenue. In this area, often referred to as 'Tin Pan Alley', offices of music publishing companies were packed wall to wall.[15] In some rooms, songwriters were writing tunes at a piano, and in others lyricists were trying to come up with new catchy phrases. Tin Pan Alley came to represent the entire pop music industry of its day. Tin Pan Alley publishers produced songs and promoted them as commodities. They contracted composers to write songs that reflected the topics of the day and to imitate the latest hits. Publishers used different techniques to promote and market the songs, with vaudevillians playing a major role in their efforts. Music publishers aggressively marketed their products to vaudeville performers in a number of ways; for instance, via ads in the trade newspaper and via 'song-pluggers' who tried to persuade variety performers to pick up the new songs (Barfe 2004; Poe 1997).

The new sound-recording technologies developed during the later years of the nineteenth century, primarily by Edison, Columbia and Victor, challenged the incumbent industry structure and changed the core product of the music industry from printed sheet music to shellac disks. Initially, these three companies considered musical content as merely a means for promoting the sales of gramophones, but during the 1920s the focus was more and more turned towards the musical content and away from the hardware.

Between them, Edison, Columbia and Victor more or less

defined the role of the 'record company'. They chose to include as part of their businesses the tasks of finding and developing new musical personalities, as well as those of manufacturing, marketing and distribution of the physical products. The music publishers, which previously had been such important actors in the music industry, were reduced to administering copyrights of composers and lyricists and to collecting royalties from the sales of records and other kinds of music-licensing.

During the 1930s and 1940s the music industry continued to be moulded by societal and technological developments. The three original major music firms evolved through mergers, bankruptcies and acquisitions into a new trio: RCA/Victor, EMI and CBS Records. These three companies came to dominate the international music industry during the following decades. A few new record companies (e.g., Decca, Mercury and Capitol) joined the trio during this period, but the overall structure largely continued to be characterized by a relatively high level of concentration at the top.

At the end of the 1950s and during the 1960s the consolidated structure of the music industry was shaken to its foundations. The development is usually explained by reference to the advent of rock 'n' roll music in concert with changes in the broadcast media environment. First, although the major firms successfully signed a number of significant rock 'n' roll acts, the new genre enabled smaller innovative firms to become at least temporarily commercially successful at the expense of their larger competitors. Second, in broadcast media, the growth of the television medium forced radio stations to revise their programming. In order to face the competition from the new medium, radio turned to music in order to get access to popular content for free, or at a low price.

One important consequence of the evolution of the broadcast media was the establishment of the radio medium as the music firms' most important promotional tool. By exposing their music in the broadcast media, they encouraged the audience to purchase the same music they had just heard in the record stores.

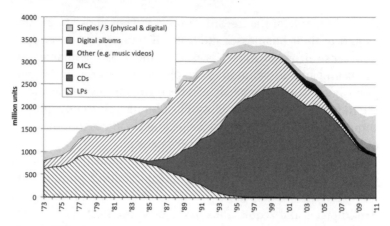

Source: IFPI 2012a

Note: It is common IFPI practice to divide singles sales numbers by three in order to make them more comparable to full-length albums. 'Other' formats include music videos (DVD, VHS, etc.) as well as Super Audio CDs (SACD), Minidiscs (MD), etc. Digital singles are included in singles sales from 2004.

Figure 2.5   Global music sales by format, 1973–2011

This straightforward business model, which was established in the mid-1950s, prevailed for several decades, and was not challenged until the arrival of Internet-based music distribution technologies at the very end of the last century.

The development of digital technology during the 1990s generated unprecedented growth in worldwide sales of recorded music. Figure 2.5 illustrates this long period of growth and how the market peaked in 1998. This expansion during the latter half of the 1980s and the early 1990s is linked primarily to the advent of the CD in 1982, which, until recently, was the dominant music distribution format. The new technology generated a boost to music sales as it motivated consumers to replace their LP collections with CDs. The recording industry has tried to repeat this feat several times since by introducing other physical distribution technologies, such as digital audio tapes (DAT), digital compact cassettes (DCC) and minidiscs (MD). However, none of these new technologies has been particularly successful; it would seem that the 'replacement effect' caused by the CD technology was a unique event that it would be difficult to replicate ever again.

Since 1998, global CD sales have been on a steady decline and the rise in online revenues has not yet been able to compensate for the loss. To date, digital technologies and the Internet have proved to be more of a challenge to than an opportunity for the music industry. The increase of online music piracy has been identified as one of the main reasons for the drop in sales since 1999. It is of course extremely difficult to establish a causal link between online piracy and declining industry sales (I will return to this issue later). What is clear, however, is that unauthorized file-sharing over peer-to-peer (P2P) networks that do not remunerate artists, composers, producers or rights holders, while potentially violating copyright laws, have thrown into question the very existence of the traditional music business model.

Subsequent chapters will delve deeper into the details of how the recorded music industry has been affected and has responded to digital technologies, but at this stage we can merely conclude that the overall impact of the digital technologies on the recorded music industry has been cost-cutting, industry-wide layoffs, consolidation, shrinking budgets for development of new acts and significant cuts in artist rosters.

If this brief account of the history of the recorded music industry has shown anything, it is how the industry is intrinsically connected to the development of technologies for the recording and dissemination of music. As a final illustration of this point, Figure 2.6 lists some of the more significant milestones in the evolution of music related technologies.

Majors and indies in the recording industry

The developments presented in the previous section have cultivated an industry structure characterized by a small number

1877	Edison demonstrates the cylinder phonograph.
1887	Emile Berliner granted patent for the disc gramophone.
1906	Victor introduces the Victrola, the first successful mass-market phonograph.
1925	The Victor Company releases the first commercial electrical recording.
1948	Columbia introduces the 33 RPM record.
1949	RCA introduces the 45 RPM record.
1958	Audio Fidelity releases the first commercial stereo record.
1964	Philips presents the Compact Cassette tape (CC) format.
1979	Sony offers a personal tape player called the Soundabout, the first Walkman.
1982	Sony and Philips introduce the compact disc (CD) format.
1989	MP3 compression technology patented by Fraunhofer Institute in Erlangen, Germany.
1993	IUMA (Internet Underground Music Archive) opens.
1998	Portable MP3 players developed by Diamond Multimedia and SaeHan Information Systems.
1999	Shawn Fanning launched the first popularized file-sharing peer-to-peer network, Napster.
2001	Rhapsody launches the first flat-fee, all-you-can-eat, music subscription service.
2001	Apple launches the iPod.
2003	Apple launches the iTunes Music Store.
2007	Streamed and on-demand music becomes part of the Billboard Hot 100 chart formula.
2008	Spotify launched its service in Sweden, Norway, Italy, Germany, France, Spain and the UK.

Figure 2.6   Milestones in the development of music distribution technologies and services

of multinational companies controlling a substantial part of the global recorded music market.

A distinguishing characteristic of these major music companies has traditionally been their control of considerable resources for manufacturing and distributing physical records.

As has previously been discussed, such dominant record companies have been referred to as 'majors' while all other smaller
companies were referred to as 'independents' (indies). In the
digital age, as resources for manufacturing and physical distribution have become increasingly irrelevant, the two terms have
remained, primarily to distinguish the largest music companies
from all the other ones. However, the terms are far from clear
and undisputed. For instance, even EMI Group often referred to
itself as the 'world's largest independent music company' (EMI
2008).

The links between indies and majors have always been strong.
Since indies are often able to accept a higher level of risk than the
larger companies, they have pioneered new artists, genres and
sounds that have not fitted into the majors' mainstream thinking. When an artist who is signed to an indie label has grown to
a certain level, it is common that a major acquires either the artist's contract or the entire label, in order to get access to the talent
and to take it to the next level. (The relationship between indies
and majors is also discussed in chapter 4.)

Since the middle of the last century, the majors have developed the practice of acquiring talents from smaller labels into a
well-established innovation strategy. In the early 1950s, major
record labels primarily comprised a monolithic and hierarchical
organizational structure that had been common practice since
the earliest days of the industry. Most of the crucial decisions
regarding the development of new talents and products were
concentrated in a group of men at the top of the organization.
These decision-makers were prone to promote their own established talents rather than to look for new talents and new forms
of expression.

Due to this proclivity for the old, the majors initially were very
hesitant about the new sounds of rock 'n' roll and rhythm 'n'
blues during the 1950s, and were convinced that the fads would
soon blow over. As time progressed, they slowly started to realize
that the sounds were there to stay. One of the first signs of the
majors' change of mind, and also one of the largest acquisitions

during the period, was RCA's acquisition of the Elvis Presley contract from Sun Records in 1953 for $35,000. While none of the other majors had succeeded in staying in the charts during the 1950s, this single acquisition enabled RCA to remain.

The 1950s and 1960s taught the majors a lesson of how not to deal with changes in the audience's preferences. To address the problem, many major record companies changed their relationship with the smaller labels. Rather than considering the indies as threats and something that should be driven out of business as quickly as possible, they began to build business relationships with them. The majors realized that the indies were able to find new artists and genres much more efficiently than they could themselves. By signing so-called 'upstream' deals with the indies, the majors had the option of acquiring contracts with promising talents, or of entering into partial ownership with the label, or sometimes even acquiring the label altogether.

The relationship between the indies and the majors continued to evolve during the 1970s. When a major acquired a smaller label, it was not dissolved within the acquirer's organization as in the old days. Rather, the acquired firm was given a considerable level of freedom and was able to continue its operations almost as before the acquisition. One example of such an acquisition and innovation strategy is the formation of Warner Records. During the 1970s and the early 1980s, Warner Communications made deals with close to 30 record labels, either through acquisitions or through alliances, and created a loosely held recording powerhouse where the creative decision-making was, to a great extent, decentralized. As long as the sub-labels delivered the expected financial results, they were more or less allowed to make their own decisions concerning the label's artist portfolio. 'The Warner model' enabled the majors to adapt quickly to changes in the audience's preferences. As evidence of the model's capability, since the 1960s, new genres such as disco, metal, grunge, rap, hip-hop, etc. have all been quickly picked up by the majors and turned into profitable styles (see Bruck 1994).

During the 1990s, the upstreaming strategy was developed a step further. When it had been introduced in the 1950s and 1960s, the majors continued to scout unsigned talents, which, over a number of years, could be developed into major talents and profitable products. Since then, such scouting activities have been radically reduced, and now almost the entire talent development capability of the recording industry resides within the smaller record companies. The majors await the development of the talents signed by the indies, and offer upstream deals to those that seem to be ready to be taken to the next level. The other internal change at the major record companies relates to the level of centralization of creative decision-making. As a result of the shrinking levels of record sales, the majors have tried to reduce costs by grouping their labels into groups that share and coordinate different resources and processes. Some label groups still allow the internal labels a considerable degree of freedom, while others are more or less a single organizational entity that runs the labels as a number of brands or product categories. As a result, rather than having a large number of labels (30-plus) within the organization which compete against each other, most majors now have only a handful of well-coordinated label groups. Whether this structure is still able to cope with the rapidly changing preferences of audiences, or whether the record companies will again end up in the same situation as during the 1950s, remains to be seen.

The current size and structure of the international music market

There is a lack of unbiased and reliable data sources that are able to give a trustworthy picture of the music industry. More often than not, it is necessary to rely on reports from consultants and music firms and publications from trade organizations. One should definitely have reservations about such data but, due to the lack of other options, the data presented below is nevertheless based on such sources.

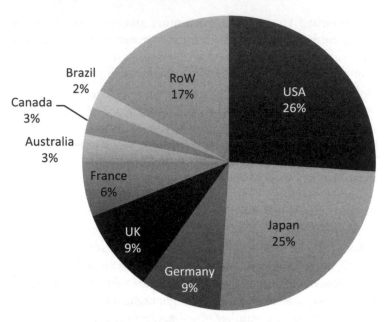

Source: IFPI 2012a

Figure 2.7   Share of the global recorded music market

The International Federation of the Phonographic Industries (IFPI) estimated that in 2012 the trade value of the global recorded music market stood at $16.5 billion, which should be compared to $28.6 billion in 1999 (IFPI 2013). In 2011, the majors jointly controlled approximately 75 per cent of the aggregate global market (Informa 2012), a number that has stayed relatively stable during the turbulent years since the turn of the century.

Since the early 2000s, the global recorded music market has been concentrated in five countries – namely, the US, Japan, the UK, Germany and France (see Figure 2.7). Combined, these five territories constitute approximately three-quarters of the global market. The US is the largest music market with a trade value during 2011 of $4.4 billion (IFPI 2012a). However, since the physical music market in Japan has proven to be more resilient than in the US, the gap between the two markets is shrinking. Japan is actually the biggest market for physical music sales, with the US market standing in second place. It should be noted that although some other markets might be large and important, it can, for various reasons, be difficult to get useful data for these areas. One such market is China, where it is estimated that almost all recorded music sold is illegal and consequently very difficult to monitor (IFPI 2012b).

To a great extent, the international market is controlled by the multinational majors, but at the same time, like most other media markets, it is not a single coherent worldwide market. Rather, it consists of a large number of distinct local markets, and music firms have to adapt their content to the local taste of each market (see, e.g., Aris & Bughin 2005). Although the majors certainly have the capacity to develop and maintain worldwide brands of selected artists, domestic artists without an international following are also of considerable importance to their businesses. In 2006, the domestic music repertoire accounted for 44 per cent of an average country's total recorded music sales, and, on a worldwide aggregated level, more than two-thirds of the global recorded music sales were generated from the domestic music repertoire (IFPI 2007). Domestic music is of considerable importance to the industry, but the specific level of importance varies both in space and in time. First, the percentage of total sales constituted by domestic music ('domestic music share') varies considerably between different countries (see Table 2.3). In some countries the value is less than 10 per cent, while in others it is more than 90 per cent (IFPI 2007). Second, global music sales declined by approximately 21 per cent between 1999 and 2006, but sales of international repertoire lost 28 per cent while the corresponding value for domestic repertoire was less than 13 per cent (IFPI 2007). In other words, it seems as if music created by domestic artists is more resilient to online piracy than music created by artists from countries far away (Picard &

Table 2.3 The domestic music share of the world's 42 largest music markets			
Country	DMS*	Country	DMS
New Zealand	9%	Spain	41%
Switzerland	10%	Hong Kong	42%
Austria	12%	Argentina	43%
Belgium	17%	Germany	45%
Chile	20%	Italy	46%
Malaysia	20%	Mexico	46%
Canada	21%	Finland	47%
Netherlands	21%	UK	50%
Ireland	23%	Czech Rep.	52%
Singapore	25%	Taiwan	55%
Portugal	25%	Greece	57%
Australia	26%	France	57%
Norway	27%	Indonesia	58%
Colombia	29%	South Korea	61%
South Africa	32%	Russia	69%
Sweden	35%	Thailand	70%
Poland	35%	Brazil	71%
Philippines	37%	Japan	75%
Denmark	39%	Turkey	87%
Hungary	39%	India	90%
China	40%	USA	93%

*Domestic music share – i.e., the percentage of recorded music sales, in a country, which was recorded by domestic artists.

Source: IFPI 2007

Wikström 2008). Data on domestic music share is unfortunately only reported for physical sales and, given that for a number of years now, online sales have constituted a substantial part of the total market, it is no longer possible to use this data in order to study the balance between domestic and international music sales.

Presentation of the world's largest music companies

The dominant multinational music companies are extremely important in the development of most aspects of the music industry. This section will give a brief presentation of the major companies in recorded music, music publishing and live music. In total, six companies will be presented. The companies are the three record company majors (Universal Music Group, Sony Music Entertainment and Warner Music Group), the publisher Sony/ATV Music Publishing and the live music production company Live Nation Entertainment. In addition, EMI Group will be presented as a separate company, even though Citigroup – the owner of the company – agreed during 2011 to sell EMI's publishing business to an investment group led by Sony/ATV and EMI's recorded music business to Universal Music Group.

Each company will be described through a short background, a panel with some current data and, when relevant, a graph illustrating the major mergers and acquisitions that have resulted in their current organizational structure. It should be noted that in these turbulent times, there are frequent mergers, spin-offs and acquisitions taking place, and the structure, client/artist roster and sizes of these companies can change from one month to another.

Universal Music Group
Universal Music Group (UMG) is the world's largest record company, controlling around 28 per cent of the official global music market (Informa 2012). UMG is part of the French media conglomerate Vivendi, but is headquartered in New York City. UMG has two main business areas: publishing and recorded music; but it also has other business units such as Bravado, the merchandising division and UMG Distribution. The organization has evolved over the decades through large and small mergers and acquisitions, as illustrated in Figure 2.8. As a result of the 2007 acquisition of the music publishing entity from the

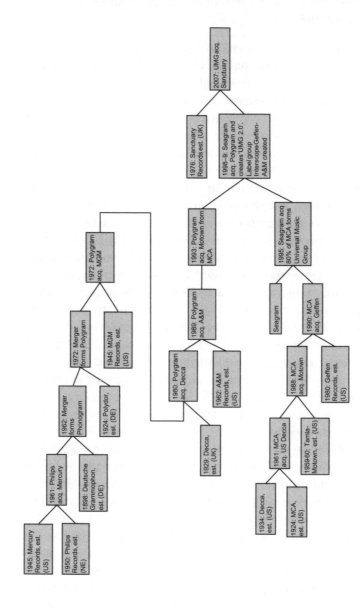

Figure 2.8   Noteworthy mergers and acquisitions during the development of Universal Music Group

German media conglomerate Bertelsmann, UMG established itself not only as the world's largest record company but also as the world's largest music publisher.

During the autumn of 2011, UMG announced that it had agreed to acquire EMI Music from Citigroup for $1.9 billion. After lengthy deliberations and negotiations, the American and European competition authorities accepted the deal in 2012 on condition that that UMG divest itself of several significant assets in its portfolio. However, even on these terms, the acquisition of EMI Music is bound to strengthen UMG's position as the world's largest record company. Figure 2.9 lists some data on Universal Music Group from 2012.

U N I V E R S A L   M U S I C   G R O U P

Company: Universal Music Group (record company and music publisher)

Headquarters: Santa Monica and New York City, USA

Global presence (2012): Offices in 72 countries.

Parent company (2012): Vivendi, France (100%)

Management (2012): Lucian Grainge (CEO)

Employees worldwide (2010): 6,967 (7,915 in 2007)

Revenues (2011): €4.2b (€4.9b in 2007)

Operating income (2011): €507m (€624m in 2007)

Global market share, recorded music (2011): 28%

Global market share, music publishing (2011): 22%

Controls record labels such as: A&M, Decca, Def Jam, Geffen, Interscope, Island, Lost Highway, Machete, Mercury, Motown, Verve

Represents artists and songwriters such as: Bryan Adams, Akon, Erykah Badu, Beck, Justin Bieber, Björk, The Black Eyed Peas, Mary J. Blige, Bon Jovi, Busta Rhymes, Mariah Carey, Sheryl Crow, Duffy, Melissa Etheridge, Feist, 50 Cent, Florence + The Machine, PJ Harvey, India.Arie, Elton John, The Killers, Lady Gaga, Lil Wayne, LMFAO, Madonna, Maroon 5, Metallica, M.I.A., Nicky Minaj, Ne-Yo, Rihanna, The Rolling Stones, Snow Patrol, Sting, Tokio Hotel, U2, Robbie Williams, Stevie Wonder

---

Figure 2.9   Universal Music Group, 2012

Sony Music Entertainment

Sony Music Entertainment is the world's second-largest recorded music company, holding approximately 22 per cent of the official global recorded music market (Informa 2012). The company was formed as a 50/50 merger (called Sony BMG) in 2004, between Sony Music Entertainment and Bertelsmann's music division, BMG. In October 2008, Sony Corporation acquired Bertelsmann's 50 per cent share in the company and changed the name back to Sony Music Entertainment.

Sony Music Entertainment was established when Sony acquired CBS at the end of 1987 as a strategic move into the content business. The consumer electronics industry and the entertainment industry have always been very close, and, by controlling assets in both, Sony hopes, among other things, to be able to control the development of new information-storage formats. Over the years, Sony has had both good and bad experiences of format battles, including the Betamax failure and the success of the Compact Disc. Sony has also tried to launch several other physical carriers and formats such as DAT, Minidisc, UMD and Blue Ray.

Figure 2.10 lists some data on Sony Music Entertainment from 2012. The history of Sony Music, visualized as a series of acquisitions and mergers, is illustrated in Figure 2.11.

Warner Music Group

The Warner Music Group (WMG) was formed in 2004 when Time Warner liquidated corporate assets and sold the Warner Music division (record labels and publishing division) to a private investment group led by Edgar Bronfman, Jr. Warner Music was listed on the New York Stock Exchange in 2005 and is now the world's third-largest music conglomerate, holding approximately 15 per cent of the official global recorded music market (Informa 2012). Since the Bronfman acquisition, WMG has been through a difficult restructuring process in which 30 per cent of their artist roster has been cut, and those artists who did not sell enough were dropped. They have also terminated

---

S O N Y   M U S I C   E N T E R T A I N M E N T

Company: Sony Music Entertainment (record company)
Headquarters: New York City, USA
Global presence (2012): Offices in 43 countries.
Global market share, recorded music (2011): 22%
Parent company (2012): Sony Corporation, Japan (100%)
Management (2012): Doug Morris (CEO)
Controls record labels such as: Arista, Bluebird Jazz, BNA, Burgundy, Columbia, Epic, J Records, Jive, LaFace Legacy, Masterworks, Provident, RCA, RCA Victor, Windham Hill, Zomba
Represents artists such as: Celine Dion, Bob Dylan, Foo Fighters, Kenny G, Alicia Keys, Avril Lavigne, Leona Lewis, Sarah McLachlan, Elvis Presley, Eros Ramazzotti, Santana, Shakira, Frank Sinatra, Bruce Springsteen, Rod Stewart, Justin Timberlake

---

Figure 2.10   Sony Music Entertainment, 2012

contracts with megastars such as Madonna, who had been signed by the company during most of her career. There have been some signs that the company is moving in the right direction. For instance, between 2004 and 2008, the sales of recorded music from the other three major music companies declined by percentages with two-digit numbers, while WMG was actually able to increase its sales by 5 per cent (Lowry 2008). However, in spite of this seemingly positive development, the company market value has plummeted since 2005, and in 2011 it was delisted as Len Blavatnik's investment firm Access Industries acquired the company for $3.3 billion.

Figure 2.12 lists some data on Warner Music from 2012. The history of Warner Music, visualized as a series of acquisitions and mergers, is illustrated in Figure 2.13.

EMI Group
EMI was acquired in 2007 by the private equity firm Terra Firma Capital Partners for $4.7 billion. After assuming control of the company, Terra Firma delisted the EMI Group's shares from the London Stock Exchange and started a massive restructuring of

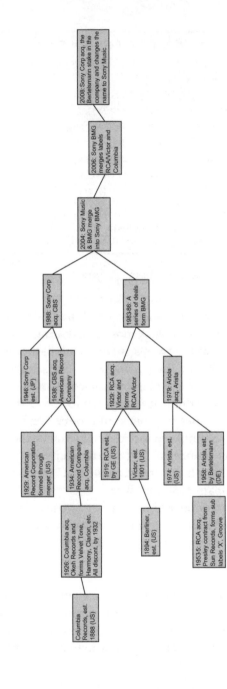

Figure 2.11   Noteworthy mergers and acquisitions during the development of Sony Music

---

W A R N E R   M U S I C   G R O U P

Company: Warner Music Group (record company and music publisher)

Headquarters: New York City, USA

Global presence (2012): Offices in 41 countries.

Parent company (2012): Access Industries, USA (100%)

Management (2012): Stephen Cooper (CEO)

Revenues (2010): $3.0b ($3.5b in 2008)

Operating income (2010): $348m ($207m in 2008)

Global market share – recorded music (2011): 15%

Global market share – music publishing (2011): 14%

Controls record labels such as: Asylum, Atlantic; Bad Boy, Cordless, Elektra, East West, Lava, Maverick, Nonesuch, Reprise, Rhino, Sire, Warner Bros., Word

Represents artists and songwriters such as: Eric Clapton, Green Day, Dr. Dre, George and Ira Gershwin, Faith Hill, Madonna, Morrissey, Nickelback, Cole Porter, Laura Pausini, Red Hot Chili Peppers, Rob Thomas, Led Zeppelin

---

Figure 2.12   Warner Music Group, 2012

EMI that included firing senior staff and selling off numerous corporate assets. During the restructuring process, EMI had serious difficulty keeping some of its most valuable artist contracts – for instance, Radiohead, The Rolling Stones and Paul McCartney all decided to leave the label during the process (Parrack 2008). In addition to the operational difficulties, EMI also had severe financial difficulties and, in 2011, Terra Firma was forced to hand over EMI to the bank (Citigroup) that funded the 2007 deal. During the autumn of 2011 Citigroup announced that it had decided to split up EMI and sell the publishing arm to an investment group led by Sony/ATV and the recorded music business to Universal Music Group. As already mentioned in the section on Universal Music, during 2012 both acquisitions were approved by the relevant competition authorities in Europe and America. As a consequence of these deals, there are now only

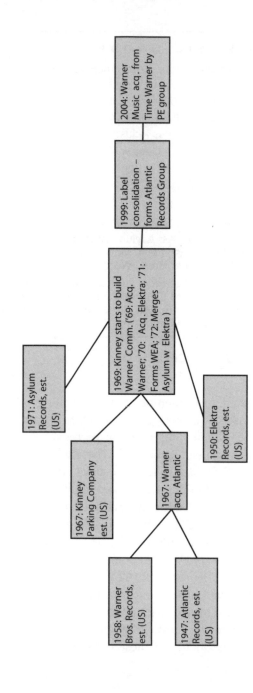

Figure 2.13   Noteworthy mergers and acquisitions during the development of Warner Music Group

E M I G R O U P

Company: EMI Group (Music publisher and record company)

Headquarters: London, UK

Global presence (2011): Offices in 50 countries.

Parent company (2011): Citigroup Inc.

Management (2011): Roger Faxon (CEO)

Global market share – recorded music (2011): 11%

Global market share – music publishing (2011): 20%

Revenues (2010): £1.65b (£1.5b in 2007)

Operating income (2010): £334m (£164m in 2007)

Controls record labels such as: Angel, Blue Note, Capitol, Mute, Parlophone, Virgin

Represents artists and songwriters such as: ABBA, Louis Armstrong, Arctic Monkeys, Richard Ashcroft, Anita Baker, The Beach Boys, The Beatles, Natasha Bedingfield, James Blunt, Blur, David Bowie, Sarah Brightman, Kate Bush, Coldplay, Phil Collins, Count Basie, Daft Punk, Dandy Warhols, Miles Davis, Depeche Mode, Duran Duran, Earth Wind & Fire, Fats Domino, Gorillaz, Ed Harcourt, Iggy Pop, Iron Maiden, Janet Jackson, Norah Jones, Alicia Keys, Kraftwerk, Lenny Kravitz, Kylie, John Lennon, Massive Attack, Paul McCartney, Moby, Nirvana, Pet Shop Boys, Pink Floyd, Judas Priest, The Prodigy, Queen, Radiohead, Cliff Richard, The Rolling Stones, Rod Stewart, Sting, Usher, Kanye West, White Stripes, Pharrell Williams, Stevie Wonder

Figure 2.14   EMI Group, 2012

three major record companies still in business. EMI has been significantly streamlined during recent years, and before the split-up of the company it was actually a profitable business. Its music publishing business was especially strong, and EMI held the position as the world's second-largest music publisher (19 per cent market share). The recorded music market had not been equally successful and controlled no more that 10 per cent of the global recorded music market (Informa 2012).

Figure 2.14 lists some data on EMI Group from 2012. The history of EMI Group, visualized as a series of acquisitions and mergers, is illustrated in Figure 2.15.

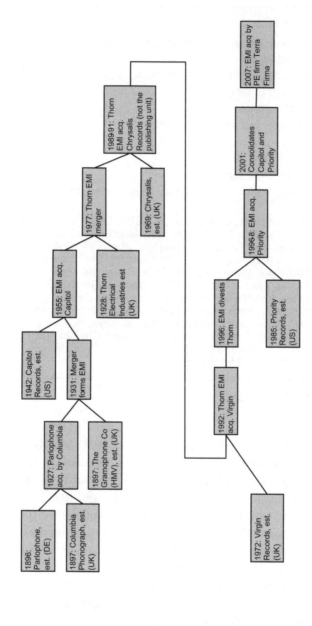

Figure 2.15   Noteworthy mergers and acquisitions during the development of EMI Group

Sony/ATV Music Publishing
Although the music publishing units at Warner, Universal and EMI are bigger than Sony/ATV Publishing, it is nevertheless the world's largest stand-alone music publishing company with a 12 per cent market share (Informa 2012). It was formed in 1995 through the merger between ATV Music, which Michael Jackson had acquired in 1985, and Sony's publishing arm. One of the most valuable possessions in the Sony/ATV catalogue is the Northern Songs catalogue, which mainly consists of 180 songs written by the Beatles. The Beatles had formed Northern Songs in 1963 together with their publisher Dick James and their manager Brian Epstein. In a series of unfortunate events, the Beatles lost control of Northern Songs when Associated TeleVision (ATV) acquired a majority stake in the company in 1969. Neither the Beatles nor managers Lee Eastman and Allen Klein were able to prevent ATV from becoming majority stockholders in Northern Songs. Losing control of the company, John Lennon and Paul McCartney elected to sell their share of Northern Songs while retaining their writers' royalties.

Sony/ATV was not a part of the 2004 joint venture between Sony and BMG, but, as previously mentioned, it is leading an investment group that has acquired EMI Music Publishing. Sony/ATV has announced that EMI Music Publishing will continue to operate as an independent unit, but, with the two publishing powerhouses combined, they will control more than 30 per cent of the market and will thereby become the world's largest publishing company.

Figure 2.16 lists some data on Sony/ATV Music Publishing from 2012.

Live Nation Entertainment
Live Nation Entertainment (LNE) has already been briefly presented in this chapter. It is a global live music giant that is more than twice as big as AEG Live, the second-largest player of the segment.

S O N Y / A T V   M U S I C   P U B L I S H I N G

Company: Sony/ATV Music Publishing (Music publisher)

Headquarters: Santa Monica, USA

Global presence: Offices in 40 countries.

Global market position: #4

Revenues (2011): $1.9 billion

Parent company (2012): Sony, Japan (50%), The Michael Jackson estate, US (50%)

Management (2012): Martin Bandier (CEO)

Administers or owns works by artists/songwriters such as: Babyface, The Beatles, Brooks & Dunn, Leonard Cohen, Miles Davis, Neil Diamond, Bob Dylan, The Everly Brothers, Jimi Hendrix, Sarah McLachlan, Joni Mitchell, Graham Nash, Willie Nelson, Roy Orbison, Stephen Stills, Hank Williams

---

Figure 2.16   Sony/ATV Music Publishing, 2012

The company was formed in January 2010 through the merger between the ticketing sales company Ticketmaster and the concert producer Live Nation (which in turn was spun off from Clear Channel Communications in December 2005). LNE is a vertically integrated company, which has booking rights for, or equity stakes in, 133 venues around the world, including the Fillmore in San Francisco and the House of Blues music venues. Besides being one of the world's largest venue operators, LNE is the world's leading promoter and during 2011 was involved in 22,000 events and sold more than 47 million tickets to various live music events. In 2011 the company generated $5.4 billion in revenues from its four business areas (live music, venue, ticketing and artist management).

While most companies in the recorded music area shrank during the first decade of this century, LNE has been able to increase its revenues by more than 10 per cent per year since the Clear Channel spin-off. As a consequence, in terms of revenues, LNE has overtaken Universal Music Group's former position as the world's biggest music company. However, although Live

LIVE NATION ENTERTAINMENT

Company: Live Nation (Live Music Company)

Headquarters: Beverly Hills, USA

Global presence: Offices in 18 countries.

Global market position: #1

Parent company (2012): Publicly traded at the New York Stock Exchange (NYSE:LYV).

Revenues (2011): $5.4b ($3.6b in 2007)

Operating income (2011): 18$m ($6m in 2007)

Employees (2011): 4,700

Management (2012): Michael Rapino (CEO)

Contracted and associated global artists include: Kenny Chesney, Madonna, Dave Matthews Band, Police, The Rolling Stones, Sting, Barbra Streisand, U2, The Who

Figure 2.17   Live Nation Entertainment, 2012

Nation is big, it has not been particularly profitable, and has lost almost 20 per cent of its value since market introduction (NYSE, December 2012). The low stock price has encouraged another US-based media giant – Liberty Media – to increase its ownership in LNE. By the middle of 2012, Liberty Media controlled about one quarter of the Live Nation shares.

Figure 2.17 lists some data on Live Nation Entertainment from 2012.

This chapter has introduced the major actors in the music industry and contextualized the ways in which the different components are connected. It has given a snapshot of how the ownership and finances of the world's major music companies have evolved during one of the most turbulent periods in the history of the music industry. The next three chapters will look more deeply into the transformation of the industry, starting with the changing relationship between music and the media.

3

Music and the Media

The three characteristics of the new music economy – high connectivity and little control, music provided as a service, and increased amateur creativity – are driven by the development of digital media technologies. Without digital media, there simply would be no Cloud. In this chapter will delve deeper into some aspects of these characteristics with a particular focus on the media as the link between music and audience. The chapter deals specifically with issues related to the promotion, licensing and distribution of recorded music. I will start out by introducing a simple model that will be able to give some structure to the reasoning and analysis. The chapter will then continue by looking specifically at how the improved connectivity impacts on the interplay between audience, media and music. From this analysis the chapter will discuss how the business of licensing recorded music has developed and it will present and discuss a number of business models for selling recorded music to consumers.

The interplay between music, audience and media

Music is an integral part of most media. Movies, radio, video-games and television all depend on music as the core or the enhancement of their products. The music industry, on the other hand, is completely dependent on the media, as a promoter, user and distributor of its products. Most professional musical artists communicate with their audience primarily via some kind of electronic medium and only a fraction of the audience is able

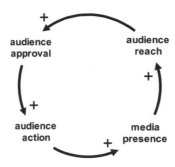

Source: Wikström 2006

Figure 3.1   The audience–media engine

to experience the artist's live performance. The dynamics of this interplay between the audience, the music and the media can be illustrated by the 'audience–media engine' model (Wikström 2006; 2009).[16] The model (see Figure 3.1) is constituted by four variables: media presence, audience reach, audience approval and audience action. Media presence represents the number of media outlets (television shows, radio shows, websites, video-games, etc.) where the artist appears during a specific period of time. A music firm may try to improve its media presence through various marketing and licensing activities. Audience reach represents the percentage of the total audience that the firm is able to reach through its media presence. For instance, an appearance in a high-profile media event is able to reach a greater share of the total audience than an appearance on a media event of less significance.

Audience approval is defined as the fraction of the entire audi-ence members who respond positively when they encounter the works of a musical artist. This variable is, of course, affected by several other factors, but the audience–media engine focuses entirely on how audience approval is driven by the artist's pres-ence in the media.

Audience approval is certainly important in both the old and the new music economy, but it is not able to pay the firm's bills.

Rather, it is various kinds of audience actions that are traditionally supposed to generate the majority of the firm's revenues. The actions spurred by the audience's approval might, for instance, be the purchase of a song, music merchandise, concert tickets or some other music-related product. However, not every action generates income; the making and posting of an 'Anime Music Video' on YouTube or somewhere else in the Cloud is a significant audience action, but it does not generate any immediate revenues for the music firm. Rather, many music firms choose to consider such actions as an infringement of their copyright terms and something that ought to be stopped entirely (these issues will be discussed further in chapter 5).

Audience action also has a feedback effect on media presence. One example from the old music economy of this feedback is the logic of the 'top 40' radio format. A radio station following this format plays the 40 most popular songs during a certain week. 'Most popular' is in this case equal to the records that have been sold the most during the previous week. In other words, audience action, in the shape of sales at record stores, feeds back to media presence, as radio airplay.

There are many other kinds of audience action, which have a similar interplay with media presence. The structure is currently manifested all over the Cloud, for instance on social network services such as SoundCloud, Facebook, etc., but other kinds of audience actions such as fan sites, blogs or college radio also adhere to the same logic.

The links that connect media presence, audience reach, audience approval and audience action constitute a reinforcing feedback loop that plays a crucial role in the music industry dynamics. The loop may serve as an engine which gives rise to (or ends) fads, brands, acts or genres. If the audience–media engine works against an artist or a music firm, it will be difficult or impossible to reach any kind of success. Similarly, if the music firm is able to get this loop to work in its favour, only the sky is the limit.

The ability to control the audience–media engine has been

at the core of music business strategy since the very beginning of the industry. The crucial questions have been: what kind of media presence is most efficiently reaching the target audience? Which media outlets should be used for promotion, and not be expected to generate any revenues? Vice versa, which outlets should primarily be used to collect revenues? What is the most efficient way to police copyright-infringing audience actions?

In the new music economy, characterized by high connectivity and little control, the logic of the audience–media engine is changed, and the music firms' crucial questions become increasingly difficult to answer. Next, I will look into this process. I will examine the background to the loss of control and discuss its impact on the media environment by introducing the concepts of 'audience fragmentation' and 'option value blurring'. I will then link these changes to the music firm by discussing the impact on the audience–media engine.

Connectivity and control

Music is an information-based product that in its core may be considered as a non-rival good. In other words, a song may be consumed, or listened to, by one person without preventing simultaneous 'consumption' by others. However, by distributing music on a piece of paper, a CD or some other kind of physical carrier, it is possible to turn music into a rival good, to create an artificial supply deficit, to control the distribution and to uphold the consumer price.

This basic principle has been supporting the music industry since the fifteenth century. Initially, sheet music was the prime vehicle for the distribution of music, and the music industry was simply just another industry among many other publishing industries such as books, magazines, newspapers, etc. It was the development of new technologies such as the piano roll at the end of the nineteenth century and, later, cylinders, disks and a plethora of other twentieth-century storage and distribution technologies that established the new industry, separated from the traditional publishing realm (see, e.g., Coleman 2003; Gronow 1983).

However, as has been discussed previously in this book, the development of the Cloud has made it significantly more difficult to convert music into a rival good. There are numerous technologies underpinning this development, such as high-speed Internet infrastructure, data compression, peer-to-peer networking, micro-payments, mobile communications and non-volatile information storage. I will not delve into the details of any of these technologies, but will merely conclude that, as a result of the development of these and other technologies, the connectivity (cf. p. 5) of the network constituted by audiences and music firms is radically improved. The barriers that previously stopped everyone, except for a few resource-rich players, from distributing information to members of the network have almost completely disappeared.

While this development has improved the audiences' access to music, it has also damaged the ability of rights holders to control the distribution of their songs on the Internet. When physical carriers become less important and Internet-based distribution gains in significance, the possibility for music firms to limit the supply of their products is rapidly diminished. This change is pervasive and irreversible. It is impossible to regain the control and limit the connectivity of the network, at least not without serious consequences for common citizens' personal integrity that few democratic governments would be willing to accept.

Audience fragmentation
As the capability to upload information to the Cloud is more widely dispersed, numerous entrepreneurs have seized the opportunity to enter the media business and launch competitors to the incumbent media outlets (see, e.g., Katz 2004; Lister et al. 2003; Thorburn & Jenkins 2003). Since the time and the resources spent by the audience on media and entertainment have not increased to the same extent, audience fragmentation

has accelerated (see, e.g., Hollifield 2003: 91; Picard 2002: 109–11; Simon 1971: 40). In practice, this means that fewer people are tuned to the same outlet, and an appearance on a specific outlet consequently reaches a smaller section of the total audience. Audience fragmentation is closely linked to the reasoning on 'increased product variety' as presented by Brynjolfsson et al. (2003) and popularized by Anderson as 'The Long Tail' (2004; 2006). Anderson refers to the development as 'a shift from mass culture to massively parallel culture' (2006: 184). For the music firm, this shift means that it has to place its acts in more outlets in order to uphold the level of media presence. The marketing department has to work harder, and has to spend more resources, to keep the audience–media engine going.

Option value blurring
In the old music economy, there existed a certain set of media outlets whose purpose was to expose the artist to the audience, and a distinctively different set of outlets that was used to collect revenues from that audience. All electronic media were considered to be members of the first set, and physical media – such as sheet music, CDs and compact cassettes – as members of the second. The fundamental logic of the old music economy rests on the assumption that 'distributing' music for free via the radio and television will stimulate the demand for the same kind of music distributed via CDs and cassettes.

One way to think about these two sets of media outlets is by using the concept of option value, introduced in chapter 1. The music firm wants the option value of the promotion-focused outlets to be high enough for consumers to be able to appreciate the qualities of the music. On the other hand, the music firm does not want the option value of these outlets to be anywhere close to the option value of the second set. Measured on an 'option value spectrum', these two sets have to be significantly distanced from each other, otherwise the consumers will not be motivated to spend money buying the same music they can get for free via another medium.

The improved connectivity that generated an increase in the number of media outlets has disrupted this old structure entirely. Cloud-based media outlets are able to vary the option value of the music they distribute ad infinitum; they are not restricted only to very high or very low levels. As a consequence, there is no longer a clear distinction between 'promotion outlets' and 'distribution outlets'. A plethora of outlets have blurred the gap between the two. Many music firms have for a long time considered Internet-based music distribution as promotion with the principal purpose of stimulating sales of the real product, primarily CDs. However, in the new music economy, it has become increasingly obvious that cloud-based music distribution not only promotes sales of music via other channels, it is also able to satisfy the music demand of a considerable part of the audience. Termed differently, the once strong link between exposure and sales is radically weakened.

Conclusively, improved connectivity has damaged the music firms' ability to control the flow of music and, of course, any other kind of digital information. As a consequence, numerous new media outlets have been launched that have increased the fragmentation of the audience and blurred the distinction between promotion outlets and distribution outlets.

Consequences for the audience–media engine
In spite of the changes discussed above, the structure of the audience–media engine remains the same and the links between media presence, audience reach, audience approval and audience action still hold. Without exposure in the media, there will be no audience action, which ultimately is what is feeding this business. However, even though the basic structure remains the same, the working of the audience–media engine in the new music economy is significantly different from in the old days.

For starters, the increased audience fragmentation affects the link between media presence and audience reach. The music firm has to expose its artists in more outlets in order to keep the audience reach on a constant level. This will require the firm to increase its marketing budgets, which in turn will have a negative impact on profitability.

Second, the music fans' improved capability to create and upload content to the Cloud means that more audience actions will contribute to the overall exposure of the artists and add to their aggregated media presence. As a consequence, music firms have to rely more on their fans in order to create a good buzz. It also means that the clever music firm does not have to increase its marketing budget in order to compensate for the raised audience fragmentation – it can also raise its media presence by supporting its fans' desire to express themselves through the music (cf. the Trent Reznor case described on pp. 1–3).

Even though more audience actions have a positive impact on media presence, there are also fewer audience actions that actually generate immediate revenues for the music firm. As was previously discussed, a posting of a remix on YouTube, a rave review on a blog or the sharing of an artist's entire back catalogue on a peer-to-peer network might have a positive impact on the accessibility and exposure of the artist. Unfortunately, it does not have an equally positive effect on the music firm's earnings. One way to solve the problem could be to rely more on businesses that are based on the artists' ability to attract the audience's attention and enthusiasm, rather than on their willingness to take out their wallets. Such businesses could, for instance, be based on advertising or on licensing. One rather unusual and controversial example of such a business was manifested by a project involving the rap artist Jay-Z and the soft-drink maker Coca-Cola during 2006. Jay-Z let an eight-minute clip from a concert at Radio City Music Hall be made available on a number of peer-to-peer networks. The clip, which was downloaded more than 3.5 million times, had a short Coke ad grafted to it, which generated exposure for the company as well as money for Jay-Z (Angwin et al. 2006).

Since the end of the 1990s, the recorded music industry has been trying to figure out how to work the unstable and out-of-control logic of their business. The Coke–Jay-Z project is merely one example of this struggle. More than 10 years into their battle, the results do not look particularly impressive. However, in spite of the rather depressing outlook for music-recording, other parts of the music industry are actually doing very well. Both the live music business and the music-licensing business have experienced several years of relatively strong growth. In addition, the audience is still passionate about music, and many entrepreneurs, primarily outside the traditional recorded music industry, experiment with innovative and promising business models that might be able to bring music to the fans and income to composers and artists.

The development of the live music sector will be discussed in the next chapter, which concerns the making of music on the stage and in the studio. In the remainder of this chapter, I will examine the two other sectors of the industry in the light of changes discussed above.

Music-licensing

Revenues from the licensing of music to various kinds of applications have always been an important part of the music business (cf. p. 58). While mechanical royalties have diminished along with the physical sales of recorded music, both performance and synchronization royalties have increased since the turn of the millennium. The graph in Figure 3.2 shows the revenues of royalty-collecting societies in the UK and the US. Since the size of the markets differs, and the revenue data are measured differently, the graph has been indexed to enable comparison. Although US data are missing for the years before 2000, the graph shows how licensing revenues have grown since the late 1990s.

One way to explain the boom in this part of the music industry is to point to the sudden increase in the number of media outlets discussed previously in this chapter. Media outlets without content are not very well equipped to attract audiences. Hence, content of some sort is required, and since music is an

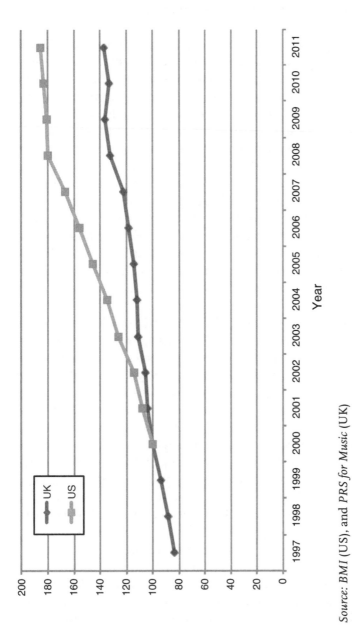

Source: BMI (US), and *PRS for Music* (UK)

Figure: 3.2   Increase in licensing revenues, 1997–2011 (Y2000: Index = 100)

integral part of most media, the demand for music-licensing has increased.

Another explanation could be a change in music firms' business strategies. As audience fragmentation and other changes in the media environment make the traditional tools for music marketing and promotion less useful, music firms' marketing departments have become more interested in the use of licensing as a means to increase record sales. The licensing of a song to an advertising campaign or to a film soundtrack may achieve considerable media presence instantly. A high-profile Hollywood production aimed for the big screen usually has a marketing budget that is considerably larger than the resources allotted to album projects of even the greatest of music superstars. Such resources are often able to turn rather feeble soundtracks into commercial successes. In the advertising space, music has become an increasingly important ingredient in the production of television commercials. One example of a significant event in the history of music in advertising is the licensing of the Rolling Stone's 'Start Me Up' for almost €10 million to promote Microsoft's operating system Windows 95 worldwide (in 1995) (Graff 2003). Another example is Apple's use of Leslie Feist's '1, 2, 3, 4' in its 2007 iPod advertising campaign. The creative use of a song in advertising can also launch an artist's career, as was the case for José Gonzalez when his version of the song 'Heartbeats' was used for the Sony Bravia 'bouncing balls' commercial. Today, the days of traditional jingles is long gone, and music is now an integral component of most advertising campaigns (Korte 2005). This increased interest from advertisers and advertising agencies has established the licensing of music to commercials as a viable promotional tool. Regardless of whether the song is old or new, the media presence generated by the licensing of the song to a television commercial is hard to overestimate.

Another medium, which has grown in importance as a music licensee, is the videogame. By mimicking their predecessors in the film industry, videogame producers have started to create soundtracks and license music to enhance their productions (see, e.g., Schnur 2005). Black Eyed Peas, Franz Ferdinand, Good Charlotte and Pussycat Dolls are all examples of acts where a videogame has been used as an important promotional platform. A marketing manager from the videogame industry compares the marketing muscles of a global videogame brand to MTV: 'If we licensed a song in our game it will be heard up to 700 million times . . . we really provide more marketing value to a record label than MTV would do with a video . . . and our licenses are all worldwide.'

The final example of media that have created new opportunities for music-licensing is mobile telephony. The significance of the mobile phone as a 'lifestyle gadget' has grown considerably since the introduction of the technology a few decades ago. As with most fashion items, a mobile device serves as a means to construct and communicate an image of the owner's identity. The actual model of the device is, of course, of great importance, but other signs and objects constitute the arpeggio that is messaged to the world. Music has been able to become a part of this package, in the shape of ringtones, callback tones etc.[17] There are many varieties of these sounds (e.g., voicetones, realtones, mastertones), and in all instances, a music licence is involved. The music industry has discovered that, while young music consumers are increasingly reluctant to purchase music for listening purposes, they are willing without any hesitation to spend their money on the latest hit as a ringtone.

It is important to note that this business is completely different from the traditional music business. The sounds purchased are often (but not always) based on mainstream pop music, but the consumer need, which these personalization products and services are able to satisfy, is completely different from the need satisfied by 'ordinary' music.

It is difficult to find reliable estimates of the size of the global market for ringtones, callback tones, etc. The market research company Gartner (2011) estimated the size of this market to be $2.1 billion in 2011. Even though this number may sound impressive, it should be noted that this represents revenues from end-users and not all of it generates a music royalty payout. In addition, it should also be noted that this market peaked in 2007 and is rapidly declining as mobile technologies mature.

Music-licensing has always been an integral and lucrative part of the music business, but it has often created a tension in the relationships between music publishers and record labels. Although music is the essential factor to both of them, their aims and their business models differ. To the music publisher or the licensing department of a full-service music firm, licensing opportunities such as the ones discussed above are the bread and butter of their business. There is simply no other kind of income besides the royalties paid by the licensees. From the record labels' point of view, the licensing has a completely different purpose, and that purpose is to promote an act. The licensing fee paid by the licensee is only the icing on the cake, since the record label's core business is the selling of audio recordings (primarily CDs) to consumers. In a competition to have a song included in a film etc., the record label might be inclined to waive the fee in order to win the competition and achieve the much desired media presence.

Media outlets often play the 'promotion card' when negotiating terms of music content licensing. The media outlet argues that the music firm should waive the licence fee, since the outlet is promoting the artist and the song. A music publisher explains: '[T]his is a perennial argument that I had with MTV . . . you can argue that most uses of music are promotion, but you have to draw the line . . . you can't give it away free, and the record companies, unfortunately, are being too willing to give music away for free.'

When licensing music to a commercial, an advertiser or an advertising agency is the licensee, and often uses the same argument as a media outlet. Another music publisher reflects on the situation:

> What is happening in the advertising world is concerning . . .
> sometimes advertisers want to use very cutting edge music . . .
> and it is seen as an opportunity by everyone to break a band,

> break a new song . . . [advertisers] are beginning to turn around
> and say 'you know we are breaking your band and we shouldn't
> have to pay to use the music' . . . there never used to be any
> question that the advertiser was expected to pay for the music
> . . . but I think it has happened during the last two or three
> years.

The intense skirmishing in the licensing negotiations has so far
not shown any signs of subsiding. It is interesting to note that
even in those cases where the music publisher and the record
label are parts of the same organization, conflicts are just as
prevalent.

The diminishing of the revenues from sales of recorded music
impacts on the negotiations between the rights holders and the
potential licensees. The licensees' traditional claim that the fee
should be reduced since the rights holders will earn their money
on sales of recorded music is no longer very solid. A quote from
a record label executive indicates how rights holders demand
higher royalties from media outlets to compensate for the
reduced sales of recorded music products:

> TV and radio have built their business models on the assump-
> tion that they have access to free content from content owners.
> Content owners have assumed that to be promotion for their
> physical products. However, since physical product sales are
> going down, content owners have begun to demand royalties for
> the use of their content on outlets such as radio, TV, etc.

This clash between rights holders and licensees will intensify
as the transformation of the media environment continues.
The rights holders in the music industry will most likely take
the lead in this process since their situation is a notch more
desperate than that of the media outlets. Based on the reasoning brought forward by this study, the rights holders' argument
weighs somewhat heavier than the argument from the licensees.
Consequently, when negotiating the fee for using a song in a particular setting, the potential promotional value of the exposure
should not be exaggerated. The fee should primarily be determined by the artistic value the song brings to the licensee and

should only be minutely influenced by the promotional value the exposure may bring back to the owner of the intellectual property.

Music publishers challenge the record labels' domain
The growing revenue from music-licensing changes the position and purpose of the music publisher within the new music economy. The music publishers, which for decades have been reduced to the role of the record labels' side-kick, have regained some of their original status. Several scholars predicted this process (e.g., Wallis 1995), but the change is no longer in the future; it is, rather, a matter of fact. Several observations show how the role of the publisher is changing. Besides the growing revenues from performance and synchronization royalties, it is also interesting to note how tasks that were previously a part of the record labels' domain are increasingly performed by music publishers. One such example is the control of the master recording.[18] Traditionally, music publishers have controlled the composition and the lyrics on behalf of the songwriter while the record label has controlled the actual recording on behalf of the performer. During recent years it has become increasingly common for artists to employ a music publisher to control not only the composition but also the recording. This enables the music publisher to act in new ways. The music publisher is able to license the recording for various purposes, without the need to involve a record label. Since music-licensing is the core business of the music publisher, the publisher is often more capable and motivated than a licensing department at the record label in getting the most revenue out of a certain intellectual property. A medium-sized US-based music publisher explains:

> There is a need to exploit the master side as well . . . it is not very different from the publishing side when you come to think about things as synchronization and even some new media . . . so we then have to put on our record label hat for a little while . . . so essentially it's a necessity . . . for our clients they need

someone to look after both sides and why not have us do it . . . it makes sense . . . being in control of publishing and the master side is very helpful, particularly in the new media where companies want to deal with one entity.

Control of the master recording also enables the music publisher to act as a record label in areas other than the licensing domain. The increased risk aversion among some music firms, especially record labels, has made the labels' A&R process slow and bureaucratic. Some music publishers have reacted to the record labels' revised A&R strategies by cutting the labels completely out of the loop to release the records themselves. When physical distribution is required in a project, the music publisher may contract a record label to handle distribution, but if the song is to be exclusively distributed via the Internet, no involvement whatsoever from a label is required.

Other similar trends are discernible among music publishers. For instance, when record labels are reluctant to invest in new performer talent, opportunities have been opened up to music publishers. Some publishers have decided to nourish inexperienced performers' careers in a way that is similar to traditional record label activities:

> I think you really have to go back to the days of the Brill Building years and the Tin Pan Alley, when there were no record labels because there were no records yet . . . the publishers were actually the promotional force behind the artist, because there was no medium outside the piano roll and the sheet music and it was the publishers that sort of peddled, they went door to door and promoted . . . the record labels came in and then that kind of significantly changed . . . they took over that role of peddling and promoting acts . . . and now I view it as trying to go back, to a certain degree.

Conclusively, not only is the revenue stream from the licensing business growing in importance, in addition, the role of the music publishers is changing and is challenging the traditional domain of the record labels. While the record labels are on the retreat, music publishers are on the advance, and it is no longer

obvious where the line between a record label and a music publisher should be drawn.

Recorded music

The previous section discussed how music-licensing is gaining in importance at the expense of recorded music. Today,
it is almost a matter of fact that recorded music is a declining
business and that the new music economy is primarily based
on revenues from licensing and concerts (see, e.g., Goodman
2008). However, consumers' demand for recorded music is
greater than ever. While the worldwide sales of music CDs have
dropped rapidly since 2000, the total number of songs acquired
by consumers legally or illegally via various peer-to-peer networks has dramatically increased. It is estimated that for every
track legally downloaded online, 20 songs are being illegally
downloaded from peer-to-peer networks (IFPI 2008). The question is whether it is possible to transform the 'online pirates' into
legitimate users of legal online music services. Today, there are
numerous legitimate services in the Cloud, all experimenting
with different business models and revenues models, all looking
for the 'killer app' that is able to attract the young and restless.
In this section I will look at a number of those services and
revenue models and analyse the potential sustainability of their
businesses.

Single-song download
Digital music sales during 2011 were estimated at $5.2 billion
and accounted for 31 per cent of the global recorded music
market (IFPI 2012a). There is a plethora of digital music services worldwide sharing these revenues, but one player, Apple
iTunes Store, still heavily dominates the market. iTunes is an
online service that carries millions of songs, and thousands of
apps, e-books, audiobooks, music videos, television shows and
movies in its catalogue. The service is developed and operated
by the computer manufacturer Apple, which, in 2003, under the

leadership of Steve Jobs, was able to convince all the majors to provide their music to the iTunes service. iTunes was the first service at the time to allow consumers to download single songs, unbundled from the album, without being required to sign up for a monthly subscription.

During the first years of running the service, iTunes followed a very clear strategy based on two principles: uniform pricing and system lock-in. Uniform pricing meant that every song in the catalogue was sold at the same price; in the US, for instance, this was 99 cents. This pricing structure was, of course, extremely easy to understand and to communicate, which facilitated the successful introduction of the service. The second principle is related to the fact that iTunes was and still is part of a larger business model, primarily based on the sales of Apple hardware such as the iPad, iPod, iPhone and the like. Initially, iTunes used a proprietary copy-protection technology (DRM) called Fairplay, which restricted consumers from playing the music acquired on iTunes on any portable device other than the Apple iPod. If consumers decided to switch to another non-Apple portable music player, they had to purchase the same songs all over again. This business strategy is referred to as 'system lock-in' and is aimed to make it difficult and expensive for those customers who want to change to other, competing technologies (see, e.g., Hax & Wilde 2001; Shapiro & Varian 1999).

Apple's initial strategy and well-crafted marketing campaigns reached an incredible level of success. In January 2008, music sales on iTunes constituted more than 70 per cent of the global legal online music market, with billions of songs and millions of iPods sold worldwide. At the time of writing, Apple iTunes Store is the largest music retailer in the US, even including the brick-and-mortar retailing giant Wal-Mart.

Starting in 2007, the iTunes strategy was increasingly challenged. Record labels tried to convince Apple to reconsider its pricing policy and to use a tiered rather than the uniform model. In addition, Apple's aggressive lock-in strategy was criticized by consumer organizations, governments and record labels.

In September 2007, in response to these complaints, another influential player, one of the world's largest online retailers, Amazon, entered the single-song download market. Amazon offers single tracks using a tiered pricing structure and without any proprietary DRM. Eventually, the pressure from Amazon, record labels and other parties forced Apple to abandon its initial strategy and since spring 2009 it has offered its entire catalogue – without DRM, and at different prices.

Memberships – limited download quota
While there are many advantages to the single-song download model, there are certainly other pricing models for online music. One such option is to offer a membership that allows music consumers to download a specified number of tracks per month. This is obviously not a recent innovation, but has been used many times in the traditional analogue copyright industries, in the shape of 'book-of-the-month clubs', 'record clubs', etc. The monthly membership fees generate a more stable and predictable revenue flow compared to other product-based models such as the single-song download model. This stability enables the service provider to offer songs to their members for a significantly lower and more competitive unit price.

One online retailer, eMusic, has been using this model for several years. For various reasons eMusic has not been able to grow at the same rate as the market for digital music, but the service is still an illustrative implementation of the 'membership – limited download quota' model. One interesting aspect of this model concerns the royalties paid by the service provider to rights holders. While Apple iTunes and Amazon pay their suppliers based on a fixed wholesale price, eMusic pays rights holders based on a revenue-sharing model. A certain percentage of the subscription revenues is added to a pool of money. These monies are then paid out to rights holders based on the number of downloads of their songs. This means that the royalties each rights holder gets varies depending on whether or not the members have used their monthly quota. Many rights holders have a rather conservative stance towards new royalty models and prefer to know in advance how much money they will earn each time a consumer downloads one of their songs. This problem, in addition to the fact that eMusic was a pioneer of DRM free music, made many major rights holders very reluctant to license their music to the eMusic service. Actually, eMusic was launched in 1995 but it was not until 2011 that it was able to license music from all the major record companies.

Memberships – all-you-can-eat
Another kind of membership model that is quite different from the one manifested by eMusic is the 'all-you-can-eat' model. This model gives members unlimited on-demand access to a large music catalogue. It is important to recognize the distinction between access-based and ownership-based models. The formal distinction between the two is that in the ownership-based models, consumers get a permanent license to listen to a song as many times as they want. The access-based models, on the other hand, give consumers access to every song in a music catalogue during a certain limited time period, for instance a month. By paying a monthly fee, consumers can listen to as many songs as they like, but as soon as they stop paying for the service, the license is terminated and they are no longer able to listen to the songs. Different versions of this model have been implemented by services such as MelOn, MOG, Rdio, Rhapsody and Spotify. Some of these services use streaming technologies, where the user has to be online in order to listen to the music.[19] Other services allow their consumers to download music, and yet other services use a combination of the streaming and downloading. The choice of technology is not very relevant from the consumers' point of view – what is far more relevant is the kind of music they can access, when they can access that music and what they are allowed to do with it.

The viability of these subscription services has been heavily debated over several years. The earliest services were not very successful and had considerable difficulties convincing both rights holders and consumers. One reason why consumers have been difficult to convince might be that they struggle with accepting the concept of a temporary licence. The illusion of being able to 'own your music', which has permeated the industry since the advent of the first recording technologies, is difficult to replace with a concept of 'music as a service' or 'music rentals'. I will return to this issue later in this chapter.

The reason why rights holders have been so sceptical about these kinds of services usually refers to the question of how to split the revenues between the owners of the copyrights. One option is to base the split on the number of downloads during a specific month – which would be identical to the eMusic revenue-sharing model. Although that principle would be clear and simple, it would not be suitable and fair for the all-you-can-eat model. It would be more appropriate to split the revenues based on which songs are currently licensed by the consumers during a specific period. A third option might be to split the revenues based on usage rather than on downloads. Assume that a consumer is curious about jazz music and downloads every jazz song she can find in the catalogue. Eventually, she learns that she only actually likes and listens to 10 of the downloaded songs; she doesn't fancy the others, and they simply remain on her hard disk drive without being touched. Based on this thought experiment, it seems fairer to split the revenues only between the rights holder of the 10 songs she likes and not between the owners of the hundreds of songs she happened to download during her discovery process. However, there is a downside to the third revenue-sharing principle, since it requires the collection of detailed usage statistics on an individual level. Since that might threaten the consumer's personal integrity, it is important that any identifier is removed from the usage data uploaded from the consumer to the service provider.

Ad-based models
All the models discussed so far are based on revenue streams directly from the music-listening audience. But these services

are not very successful in competing with the free (but illegal) services available 'two clicks away'. One way to compete with free services is to create a business model that collects revenues from sources other than the audience. If such a model is crafted in a clever way, the audience will experience the service as if the music is free, and, hence, the incentive to use the illegal services is, at least in theory, removed. 'Feels-like-free' music services are far from a new phenomenon. Traditional commercial broadcast radio stations feel like free to the consumer as they collect their revenues from advertisers rather than from their listeners.

The digital versions of these services are available in a range of flavours, all offering different option values. The vanilla flavour is basically a carbon copy of the traditional commercial broadcast radio model, merely transferred to the Internet platform. Music and any other content is not downloaded to the listener, but is streamed from the service provider. As in the case of traditional broadcast radio, the programming follows a predefined playlist, which the listener is unable to influence. Record labels have no problems getting their heads around these kinds of services. The services fit well in the old music industry logic where music was exposed in one media outlet in order to raise the demand for the same kind of music distributed via a physical carrier.

Ad-based music services, which offer an option value slightly higher than the service presented above, enable the listener to personalize the playlist in some way or another. There is a range of different mechanisms for creating personalized playlists. One option might simply be that a group of users listen to the same stream and vote for songs that they think should be added to the list (e.g., Soundrop). Other personalization mechanisms try to create a list of songs that share certain musical or technical characteristics (e.g., Music Genome Project and The Echo Nest) or a list of songs simply based on what other users who enjoy a certain song also choose to listen to (cf. the recommendation engine used by the online retailer Amazon). In addition, these personalization mechanisms are often combined with other tools that allow the users to tell the service what kind of music they like.

All in all, these technologies make it possible to create playlists that are well tuned to the tastes of specific listeners. Thereby, it is possible to create a personalized and appealing music experience even though the service lacks on-demand capability and the listener is unable to decide exactly which song should be played at a particular point in time.

Besides being able to play songs that the listeners are very likely to appreciate, the collection of the detailed usage data enables the service provider to charge a premium for targeted advertising, and thereby to increase the likelihood of the service ever reaching break-even. From the rights holders' perspective, these 'radio-like' services fit relatively well into their traditional way of categorizing various media technologies as either a promotion tool or a music distribution technology. In this case, the ad-based personalized streaming services are categorized as promotion tools and tastemakers, rather than a potential substitution to actual downloads or CD sales. However, the question is whether they really are making the correct judgement. The services are doing an excellent job as tastemakers and are in one sense stimulating the listener's music awareness. But the structure and features of the services also enable them to satisfy the listeners' music demand and to reduce the demand for the same music distributed via high-option-value technologies. These personalized Internet radio stations are illustrative examples of music services that are difficult to categorize as either promoting sales or substituting sales. The services belong to both sets at the same time.

If we continue along the option-value spectrum towards high-option-value services, we find ad-based, feels-like-free services that actually offer music on demand. Regardless of whether the distribution principle is 'download' or 'streaming', the users are able to listen to the music of their choice whenever they want. From the rights holders' point of view, this kind of on-demand music service is identical to the single-song download model. Since users are able to listen to whatever music they want, whenever they want, this is no longer a promotion tool; it must be a music distribution technology. Based on that understanding, many rights holders argue that they need a much higher compensation from the providers of on-demand music services compared to what they request from providers of playlist-based services.

Apple's iTunes agreements, which offer rights holders about 70 per cent of the retail price per download, have evolved into the industry benchmark for record label/online retailer agreements. The problem is that there are no ad-based business models that are able to generate enough revenues to cover such high licensing fees. The providers of ad-based music services try to convince the rights holders that these services should not be compared to the deals made with iTunes and the like. Rather, as the service providers claim to be able to pull the audience away from illegal file-sharing activities, they argue that the revenues from these services should be compared to zero cents per download rather than with the royalties paid by single-song download services. Based on that reasoning, rights holders ought to be happy with a revenue-sharing model, based on revenues from advertising sales.

Even though rights holders are extremely reluctant to accept that reasoning, some agreements between rights holders and providers of ad-based, on-demand music services have nevertheless been made. The majority of these agreements have so far favoured the rights holders rather than the service providers. For instance, a service provider is often required to pay a fee for each stream that is served in addition to a considerable chunk of the advertising revenues. Second, the major music firms have required an equity position in the service provider's limited company. Third, to ensure that the rights holder does not have to carry any risk whatsoever, the service provider is required to make a large prepayment from which future payments are supposed to be deducted.

To date, there hasn't been a single on-demand, purely ad-based, music service that has been successful. The European-based music service Spotify (discussed later in this chapter) is most likely the one that currently has the strongest ad-based proposition. In order to convince the rights holders to license their songs to the service, Spotify was required to abandon its original business model, which was entirely based on advertising revenues, and add a subscription-based version to the original ad-based version. It also had to structure the two versions so that users were strongly encouraged to 'upgrade' and start paying the monthly subscription fee.

From one point of view, it is certainly understandable that rights holders are reluctant to give away their valuable intellectual properties simply to allow aspiring and perhaps naive entrepreneurs to experiment with their latest music business concepts. Many experienced entrepreneurs have failed miserably in such endeavours. However, considering the development within the illegal sphere of the online music scene, and the infinitesimal likelihood of the rights holders ever being able to regain control of that sphere, it does strike me as somewhat strange that the rights holders – at least so far – have so vigorously rejected the prospect of some complementary revenues.

Cloud storage services
As the price of broadband Internet access has continued to drop, it has become increasingly feasible to store data in the Cloud rather than on a local hard disk drive. Several major technology players (e.g., Amazon Cloud Drive, Apple iCloud, Google Drive, Microsoft SkyDrive) as well as a number of start-ups (e.g., Box. net, Dropbox) have launched different types of cloud storage services. Most of them use a Freemium pricing model, meaning that they offer one advertising-funded 'free' version and a set of premium versions with additional features and without ads. The basic feature of a cloud storage is fairly simple – it allows you to upload data to a remote location and to access that data from more or less any device with an Internet access. Some of the single-song download service providers – such as Apple, Amazon and Google – have linked their online music retail stores to their cloud storage services so that songs purchased in

the store are automatically available in a personal cloud storage that the user can access via streaming from anywhere. While this is a useful but fairly basic addition to their services, it gets somewhat more interesting when cloud storage providers allow users to upload any song to the Cloud. In late 2011 Apple launched iTunes Match, a service that scans the users' iTunes local libraries and makes all the songs in a library available on Apple iCloud. iTunes Match does not ask whether the songs have been acquired via iTunes, ripped from a CD or illegally downloaded from a file-sharing service. In other words, by subscribing to the service, the users' potentially bad deeds are forgiven and they are able to listen legally to the songs they have collected in dubious ways over the years. Apple obviously has obtained the rights holders' permission to offer such a service, but that is not the case for all cloud storage service providers offering similar features. The question whether users are allowed to upload legally purchased songs to their cloud storage is not easily settled. Many rights holders argue that users do need an additional licence and have to pay an extra fee if they want to be able to access their music from multiple devices. Both major cloud storage providers such as Google and smaller players such as MP3Tunes argue that no additional license is required. It remains to be seen how the legal structures and practices for cloud storage services in different parts of the world are eventually settled.

Value-based pricing models

There are other somewhat more exotic revenue models that may or may not be realistic in the long term, but still are interesting objects of analysis. Most of these models centre on the concept of value-based pricing; that is, to charge for a service or product in relation to the value delivered to the customer. Value-based pricing is interesting when applied to the music business, since the value music gives to people may vary greatly. The song that moves one person to tears may be perceived as totally uninspiring to another. In such a scenario, how should a value-based pricing scheme be implemented?

One way to attack the issue is to ask listeners to pay whatever they think is the appropriate amount, known as the 'Tip Jar' model. If that amount is zero, then the listener does not have to pay anything at all. One small record label has tried to create a business based on this principle. The record label is Magnatune, founded by John Buckman in 2003. Magnatune split its revenues 50/50 with the rights holders whose music they offered. The record label offered the music in various kinds of packages, also as single-song downloads. The difference between this and other single-song download services was that the consumers were able to choose how much they wanted to pay for the music they downloaded, ranging between $5 and $18. The Magnatune service has been operating for a number of years, but it has not succeeded very well. One reason may be the lack of promotion, another that the music catalogue primarily consists of unsigned and relatively unknown artists. As with many of the somewhat more unusual models, the major record labels have not shown any interest in being part of the experiment.

It is highly unlikely that Tip Jar models will become anything more than a curiosity among recorded music pricing models. Even though the average price people pay will be above zero, the additional unpredictability that the model adds to the business is very appealing to the contemporary music industry.

A more viable alternative to the Tip Jar model is to offer music to consumers in differently priced packages aimed to appeal to different consumer categories. This kind of pricing strategy is normally termed 'versioning' or 'quality discrimination' and is common practice for products such as travel, software or many other cloud-based services. Airline travel is offered as economy, business or first; software as basic, home, small business or ultimate; and cloud-based information services as basic, plus or premium. In the case of music, or more particularly a specific set of songs, there are several ways to differentiate the quality of the product, such as by changing the packaging or the quality of sound, by limiting the supply or by providing access to 'extra material'. In addition, and of equal importance, the value of the

CASE STUDY: RADIOHEAD'S *IN RAINBOWS*

Radiohead is one of the world's most successful rock bands, with a career spanning more than two decades. On 10 October 2007, Radiohead had ended its contract with EMI Group and was able to decide how, where and when its newly recorded album, *In Rainbows*, should be released. Rather than releasing the album through the traditional distribution channels, Radiohead offered it as a download on its website. In a very unconventional move, the band allowed fans to pay as much or as little as they wanted for the album, including nothing at all. The Radiohead front man, Thom Yorke, explains: 'Every record for the last four – including my solo record – has been leaked. So the idea was like, we'll leak it, then' (Byrne & Yorke 2007). Interestingly, many fans did pay for the album. According to the Internet market research company comScore, the album was downloaded approximately one million times and 40 per cent of fans paid, on average, $6 for the download. This means that the average revenue per download was $2.40, which most likely is more than the share they would have received during their EMI contract.

The experiment lasted for two months and the album was released via traditional channels in January 2008. One year after being 'leaked' on the band's own website, *In Rainbows* had sold three million copies; it had reached number one spot in the US *Billboard* 200 and in the UK album chart. In 2009, the album won two Grammy Awards for Best Alternative Music Album and Best Special Limited Edition Package. Even though the experiment was probably profitable for the band, it should perhaps be considered as a promotional gimmick rather than a sustainable pricing and distribution strategy. The band's manager, Bryce Edge, explained right after the release of the album: 'In November I have to start with the mass market plans and get them under way. If I didn't believe that when people hear the music they will want to buy the CD, then I wouldn't do what I am doing. This is a solution for Radiohead, not for the industry' (Barrett 2007).

music can of course be varied by manipulating the option value. There are numerous examples of how versioning strategies are increasingly applied to the recorded music industry. One high-profile example is the Justin Timberlake album *FutureSex/ LoveSounds* released in September 2006. In all, 115 different

---

CASE STUDY: VERSIONING *GHOSTS I–IV*

The Trent Reznor case presented at the beginning of the Introduction is an example of quality discrimination, as Reznor offered the recording in five different versions:

Free The first nine tracks from the *Ghosts I–IV* collection available as high-quality, DRM-free MP3s, including the complete PDF.

$5 All 36 tracks in a variety of digital formats including a 40-page PDF.

$10 2 x CD set: *Ghosts I-IV* on two audio CDs in a six-panel digi-pak package with a 16-page booklet. Includes immediate full download in a variety of digital formats.

$75 Deluxe Edition Package: *Ghosts I-IV* in a hardcover fabric slipcase containing: two audio CDs, one data DVD with all 36 tracks in multitrack format, and a Blu-ray disc with *Ghosts I-IV* in high-definition 96/24 stereo and accompanying slideshow. Includes immediate download in a variety of digital formats.

$300 Ultra Deluxe Limited Edition Package: Includes everything you get for $75, plus an exclusive four-LP 180-gram vinyl set in a fabric slipcase, and two exclusive limited edition Giclée prints in a luxurious package. The package is limited to only 2,500, and each one is signed by Reznor himself.

---

products/versions have been created from the project, which in total has sold more than 19 million units worldwide. Only 20 per cent of these were CDs (IFPI 2008).

Bundling music with other media products

The practice of grouping products or services into a set which then is marketed and sold as a single package is referred to as 'product bundling'. The practice is common in many industries, for instance in the cable television industry, where consumers are often required to subscribe to a whole set of channels even if they are interested in only one of them. It is also common practice in the music industry where the full-length album is the well-established way to bundle a set of songs.

Another bundling model, which is becoming increasingly common, is to combine various products with specific issues of magazines or newspapers. Such 'covermounts' have developed into an important promotion opportunity for the music industry and is, likewise, an important way for the magazine publishers to enhance the value of their product. The bundling strategy is not, however, restricted only to these combinations. Recorded music is, for obvious reasons, linked to listening devices, both portable and stationary. Since 1997, when the first portable digital audio players with large non-volatile internal memory reached the market, it has become common practice to pre-load them with some kind of music. In most cases, this kind of bundling is not very sophisticated. A handful of tracks are simply pre-loaded onto the device to ensure that the consumer has something to listen to right from the start. However, some cases are more interesting. One such was the cooperation between the Irish rock band U2 and Apple. This lasted for several years and included, among other things, a commitment from U2 to participate actively in the marketing of iPod and iTunes products. However, the most visible part of the project was a specially designed iPod, engraved with the band members' autographs and bundled with all the music (400 tracks) ever recorded by U2.[20]

'Nokia Comes with Music' was another interesting (but eventually failed) bundling initiative launched in 2008 by the Finnish handset manufacturer Nokia. The programme gave people who purchased certain Nokia phones 'unlimited' access to a music catalogue during 12 months. The option value of this offering was fairly limited, since the downloaded songs were not transferable to other handsets. Nevertheless, it is notable that the songs were offered with a permanent licence and remained useful and listenable after the end of the 12-month period. To be able to offer permanent licences and unlimited access to music from all four majors, Nokia paid hefty amounts to the rights holders for every handset sold, and it is unlikely that this programme was ever intended to be profitable on a stand-alone basis. Rather, it should be seen as an aggressive way for Nokia to get a foothold in the music business. In parallel with the 'Comes With Music' programme, Nokia launched a music service by the name of Ovi,

where music, movies and other information products was supposed to be offered according to a pay-per-download model. The
purpose of the 'Comes With Music' was to get the Ovi service
off the ground. It fairly soon became evident that this bundling
initiative was unable to gain traction in the market. In early 2011,
'Comes With Music' was closed down in 27 of the 33 markets
where it was available at the time, and by the end of 2012 the Ovi
brand had been discontinued.

Nokia is not the only handset manufacturer that has shown
interest in the music business. For instance, its competitors
Samsung, HTC and, obviously, Apple all have strong interests
in the music and entertainment businesses. These initiatives are
part of a major industrial transformation whereby the technology and telecommunication industries are moving closer to the
music and entertainment industries. The next section takes a
closer look at this process of industrial convergence.

Music and the telecom industry
Since 1981, when the world's first fully automatic mobile
telephony service was launched in Scandinavia, wireless communications have come a long way. By the end of 2011 there
were six billion mobile telephone subscriptions and 1.2 billion
mobile broadband subscriptions worldwide (ITU 2011). This
new infrastructure has rapidly transformed the way people
travel, socialize, do business – and listen to music.

The two most important drivers of profits in the mobile
telephony business are the average revenue per user (ARPU) and
churn – i.e., the proportion of the subscribers who leave the service during a given time period. All mobile telephony operators
strive to keep their ARPU as high as possible and their churn as
low as possible. One way of achieving these goals is to offer the
users long-term subscription plans and add-on services which
encourage customer loyalty and stimulate users to spend their
entertainment monies through their mobile phones.

While the mobile telephony operators hunger for services
that increase ARPU and customer loyalty, the recorded music

industry is in an equally desperate position. By combining the strengths of the two industries, the hope is that both their respective wishes will be fulfilled. In the most advanced mobile telephony markets around the world – particularly in northeast Asia and in Europe – mobile operators and music companies have embraced one another. One such example is SK Telecom, the largest mobile telephony operator in South Korea with more than 24 million subscribers (2012). SK Telecom has moved into the music industry by acquiring a leading South Korean record label, JYP Entertainment, and a major Korean distributor, Seoul Records. In 2004, it launched MelOn, one of the first all-you-can-eat music subscription services bundled with a mobile telephony service. MelOn became a rapid success and it is still the leader of the Korean digital music market. In 2011 subscriptions constituted 36 per cent of the digital music market, which in turn constituted 54 per cent of the total Korean music market (IFPI 2012a). Today, an increasing number of mobile telephony operators in different parts of the world offer various music subscription services, and the music industry's dependency on revenues channelled via mobile telephony operators is consequently growing. Among the models presented in this chapter, the all-you-can-eat model is by far the most appealing one to package with a traditional mobile telephony subscription plan. For instance, it is a very straightforward task to add such a service into the mobile telephony operator's billing system, while a music service based on the single-song download model is far more complex to integrate with a mobile operator's subscription-based business structure.

Access and ownership

This chapter has presented a number of models for how recorded music can be packaged, priced and legally distributed online. We have discussed single-song downloads, feels-like-free models based on advertising revenues, different types of membership models, value-based pricing, bundling, etc. It remains to be seen which of these models will be viable in the long term and which will not. The retailers and online services currently operating in the marketplace seldom restrict themselves to a single model, but instead combine several different models in their value propositions. Such a hedging strategy allows the service providers to carefully follow what models users and rights holders prefer and to adjust their offerings accordingly. An important dividing line between different models relates to the issue of 'ownership and access', as discussed earlier in this chapter. The old music economy was based on creating a sense of ownership. I argue in this book that rights holders' ability to control the digital distribution of their intellectual properties is rapidly diminishing. As soon as some kind of information is uploaded to the Cloud, it does not take very long for it to be universally accessible. As previously reasoned, in such a friction-free network, the economic value of providing access to individual tracks is relatively close to zero. Hence, it is possible to conclude that some of the models presented above – based on ownership and control – have a relatively bleak future while others – based on access – are more sustainable. As was discussed above, 'all-you-can-eat' services of various kinds can be bundled with other kinds of media and communication services; they can be financed through various combinations of adverts and subscriptions and they can easily be structured into different versioning packages.

However, access-based models have been around for some time and, until fairly recently, they have not been very successful. Both users and rights holders find them difficult to grasp and incompatible with their traditional ways of using and distributing recorded music. There are, however, some access-based music services that seem to be quite promising. The foremost example is the already mentioned Spotify. Spotify was established by two Swedes, Daniel Ek and Martin Lorentzon, in 2006 and was launched in a number of European countries in late 2008 after lengthy and difficult negotiations with major as well as independent music companies. Ek has stated that record label executives initially bluntly refused to license their songs to the service, and that they declined even to try out the service themselves. In an attempt to show the executives why the service had to be taken seriously, Spotify offered it for free to those high schools where they knew the executives' children were enrolled. Slowly the music executives noticed how their children's use of the service had a fundamental impact on their music listening behaviour. They realized that perhaps Spotify might be able to compete with piracy and compensate the rights holders.

Spotify uses a Freemium model, which means that it has one advertising-funded 'free' version and a set of premium versions with additional features and without ads. By the end of 2012, Spotify reported it had 20 million users worldwide and that 5 million of these were subscribers paying the monthly fee. The company is still in its early days in several markets – including the US – but where it has been operating the longest (e.g., Sweden and Norway) it has quickly positioned itself as the leading 'retailer' of recorded music (IFPI Sweden 2012). The decline of recorded music sales in Sweden, which started in 2000, has been halted and since early 2011 revenues generated by recorded music in Sweden is growing, largely due to the increasing revenues from the Spotify service (IFPI Sweden 2012). The company has reported both healthy advertising and subscription revenues in these markets and an increasing number of initially sceptical rights holders have been turned around and have decided to accept Spotify's business model (Bradshaw 2012). However, even though Spotify has strong supporters and several success stories to tell, the service is still controversial in many quarters, primarily among independent artists, composers, publishers and record labels. The hard-core sceptics believe that Spotify's business model is simply a scam that may be able to generate revenues to the major record labels, but only meagre royalties to independents. They argue that the successes in the smaller markets cannot be replicated in larger markets such as the US, since the logic of those larger markets is totally different than their small tech-savvy Scandinavian counterparts. Further, they argue that the service is cannibalizing the sales via traditional formats and that the whole venture is non-viable in the long term and simply a way for shrewd venture capitalists to build a hype and make a profitable exit as soon as possible (e.g., Peoples 2012; Resnikoff 2012).

Mermigas (2006) argues that when rights holders choose emerging distribution models, they should ensure that the new models add revenues and do not cannibalize existing businesses. A number of significant rights holders seem to follow this recommendation and refuse to license their music to the service. Spotify is steadily growing and gaining traction among both users and rights holders, but it is, at the same time, struggling to stave off criticism. It still remains to be seen whether Spotify will eventually establish itself as the second music retailer next to iTunes, or if the sceptics' criticism will prove to be right. While research shows that the service is indeed able to compete with piracy (e.g., Delikan 2010), it seems as if the service is, at the same time, contributing to the continued decline of physical sales.

Surely, from this perspective the sceptical rights holders' strategy may be understandable, but their stance is undeniably also associated with a significant level of risk. By applying such a defensive wait-and-see strategy, they run the risk of being unable to respond to major shifts in their environment (cf. pp. 37–9). A more appropriate adaptation strategy might be the prospector approach, where innovation is of highest priority. In a copyright industry such as this one, the prospector approach is a far more sustainable strategy, although, in the short term, it may yield lower profit levels than the defender strategy (Miles & Snow 1978).

As the traditional recorded music business slowly deteriorates, record labels will hopefully change their stance and embrace the new music economy once and for all. There are inspiring examples from other firms that have been able to renew themselves, turn back the industry lifecycle to an earlier stage and continue their existence for several years forward. IBM is one such company that has been able to renew its business more than once during its century-long history. Lou Gerstner, the CEO who turned IBM around during the 1990s, explained their problems:

> The company didn't lack for smart, talented people. It had file drawers full of winning strategies. Yet the company was frozen in place . . . all of these capabilities were part of a business model that had fallen wildly out of step with marketplace realities . . . History shows that the truly great and successful companies go through constant and sometimes difficult self-renewal of the base business. (Gerstner 2002: 16, 176, 220)

One lesson to be learnt from the IBM case is how important it is for firms to be able to 'unfreeze' their traditional way of thinking and challenge the truths that for too long have been taken for granted. Such soul-searching is a challenging process to get through, but one through which the recorded music business has to pass.

This chapter has examined how the music business interplays with the media and how digital technologies transform that relationship. I have discussed how the industry's centre of gravity has moved away from recorded music towards other parts of the industry. I have also discussed a number of potential revenue models that might be able to work as the basis for profitable online-based recorded music businesses.

4

Making Music

This chapter focuses on how professional music-making takes place in the new music economy. The chapter will look at how the ways creative people define their occupations and organize their careers can influence the nature of the work they produce. It will explore the concept of the artist as a brand and link that discussion to the changing practices and routines related to talent development. It will also analyse developments within the live music sphere and discuss how the contractual relationships between artists and their business partners are affected by the new music industry dynamics.

Professions and practices

One of the most important characteristics of the new music economy is the ability for amateurs to express their creativity by making and publishing music in the Cloud. The distance between the amateur and the professional artist has been radically reduced. Even though content generated by users may be important to music firms, not every teenager who yearns for a place in the limelight will succeed. The combination of drive, talent and luck simply is not homogeneously distributed across the population. In the end, only an extremely small number of people will be able to make a decent living as a creative force in the music industry. But a very interesting question is, what does it mean to be a professional artist, songwriter, etc.? Is it even possible to claim that such activities are professions? These kinds of questions have been discussed by several popular music scholars – for instance, by Jason Toynbee (2000). It is clear that in the decades since the music industry entered the digital age, a powerful process of reprofessionalization has also taken place. One of the professions that has most fundamentally been redefined is that of the music producer.

The music producer

Prior to the 1950s, music-recording was a well-structured process that was carried out by people with a number of equally well-defined roles. A&R agents 'discovered' the potential talent and signed them to the label; songwriters provided the artist with new material; and the in-house studio engineers controlled the machinery and ensured that the sound met the expectations of the creatives and the marketers. During the 1950s and 1960s, this structure was challenged when a new technology entered the recording studios. This new technology, which is referred to as multitrack recording, is one of the most revolutionary audio-recording innovations (Cunningham 1999; Moorefield 2005).

Before multitrack recording, musicians and singers delivered their songs as a live band and had to make sure that it sounded at least good enough to be pressed to plastic. When someone played the wrong note or made some other kind of 'mistake', the entire song had to be re-recorded or the mistake had to be accepted as a creative interpretation of the song. Multitrack recorders changed this production process entirely, since they enabled the recording of individual instruments and voices, rather than all instruments and voices at the same time. If there was a mistake in one of the channels, that specific channel could be re-recorded without affecting all the others. Multitrack recording also made it possible to change the song quite radically, even after all the musicians and singers had left the studio. For instance, the level of voices or instruments could be changed, or specific voices and instruments could be moved around within the stereophonic audio space. In other words, multitrack recorders moved some of the creative work from the studio into the control room and into the hands of the studio engineer or the music producer.

The Beach Boys and The Beatles were two groups that stood

at the centre of the transformation from mono- to multitrack recording. At the start of their careers, they recorded their music live to mono- or two-track recorders, but in the mid-1960s both bands had access to multitrack recorders that enabled them to develop entirely new sounds and arrangements. The pioneering sounds of The Beach Boys' album *Pet Sounds* and The Beatles' album *Sgt. Pepper's Lonely Hearts Club Band* were enabled by multitrack recorders. For both bands, there are certain individuals who have been recognized as very influential creative and technical forces behind the sound – the producers. In the case of The Beach Boys, the producer was Brian Wilson; in the case of The Beatles, it was George Martin. Brian Wilson was a member of the band, but he also had the role of composer, arranger and studio engineer. George Martin was not formally a member of The Beatles, but he was so intimately involved in creating the band's sound that he is often recognized as the 'fifth Beatle'. Multitrack recording technology contributed enormously to the shaping of the modern role of the music producer, which today includes facets such as composing, A&R and hands-on work at the mixer console.

Digital audio-recording technologies have continued to shape the role and practice of the music producer. Digital technologies make it possible to sample, loop and process sounds into completely new songs, arrangements and musical genres, and the gradual shift of the locus of the creative work – from the studio to the control room – has continued and accelerated. One important aspect of digital audio-recording technologies is their ability to compensate for 'mistakes' made by musicians and singers. For instance, a couple of tones slightly out-of-pitch cause no problem at all with modern pitch-correction software, which is able to make it sound as if even the most tone-deaf singer is pitch-perfect. With digital audio-recording, it is possible to create the 'perfect' sound, with perfect pitch, perfect tempo and perfect timbre, even though the artistic raw material might not be very musically gifted.

In some genres, the music producer is the single creative force behind the musical output, and the artist has more or less been removed from the creative process. This new situation opens up fresh opportunities for the music producer with an entre-preneurial mind. One option is to cooperate with an artist who might not have the best musical abilities but who has an image and visual appearance that are able to connect with the target audience's expectations and desires. One relatively early produc-tion team that followed this strategy was the UK-based Stock, Aitken and Waterman trio who, during the 1980s and 1990s, produced a string of hits together with acts such as Bananarama, Rick Astley, Kylie Minogue, Jason Donovan, Samantha Fox and many others (Stock 2004). Some years later, a similar model was used by members of the Swedish music producer community. One example is the music producer team linked to Cheiron Studios in Stockholm, Sweden. Cheiron Studios was founded by Denniz Pop and Tom Talomma in 1992, and they were later joined by talented producers such as Andreas Carlsson, Jörgen Elofsson, Max Martin and others. These producers have provided their services to artists such as Britney Spears, Westlife, N'Sync, Backstreet Boys, Céline Dion and Bon Jovi. Even though Max Martin and friends may be superstars within the international music producer community, none of them has desired or man-aged to create a mainstream recognition that is able to compete with the fame and recognition of their superstar partners. However, there are other music producers who have taken the development of their role full circle by eliminating the artist altogether and entering the limelight themselves. For instance, there are a number of US-based music producers, especially within the R&B and hip-hop genres, who have chosen this strat-egy. Some of the most successful producers in this area are Dr Dre, Timbaland, Pharrell Williams and Jay-Z. Even though these producers have been able to build their careers independently from traditional artists, many of them still collaborate with sing-ers and musicians in various projects. This collaboration is often quite different from the traditional artist–producer relationship. Sometimes the producer is promoted as the 'host' who invites artists to be featured in different songs. In other projects the artist has a more central role, but still the producer is not in any way hidden in the studio, as was always the case in the old days, and he or she is consciously used and exposed together with the artist in music videos, promotional appearances and sometimes even live stage performances.

To conclude, the role of the music producer has, since the 1960s, been transformed from engineer to stage performer. To a large extent, this transformation has been enabled, or perhaps even determined, by various technological innovations. Audio-recording technology has become increasingly tolerant of singers' and musicians' human slips, and we have eventually reached a state where these traditional craftsmen's competences are no longer needed to create polished, flawless, recordings. This development has so far been limited to some specific genres, and the question remains whether it ever will become the *modus operandi* for all kinds of music production and recording. Music without flaws runs the risk of becoming lifeless and a bit boring. There are technologies that try to replicate human imperfections in order to make the music more lifelike, but still some music and sounds *have* to be performed by flesh-and-blood human beings for it to be bearable to listen to them. For instance, I would say that it is unlikely that the magical sounds and unique creativity of Wynton Marsalis, Michael 'Flea' Balzary, Polly Jean Harvey and their peers will ever be replicated by digital machinery.

Recording studio decline
Digital and analogue recording technologies have not only shaped the role of music producers, but also affected their workplaces: the recording studios. In the early days of recorded music, the studio was a vital and almost defining part of the record company, but independent recording studios and production companies began to emerge in parallel to the development of the music producer. However, to set up and run these professional recording studios was a fairly capital-intensive endeavour. The

physical characteristics and features of the studios had to provide excellent acoustics; the facilities had to be pleasant enough to ensure that artists were inspired or simply had somewhere to hang out while waiting for the next take; the recording equipment required major investments and continuous reinvestments in order to be up to date with the latest technological development. Consequently, most artists were unable to create their own professional music studio in their basement. When a recording project was under way, artists had no option but to turn to the recording studio and pay an hourly or daily fee to get access to the facilities and equipment on offer. The continuous and steady production of records meant that the established studios had an equally steady and predictable demand for their services. Times were good (Cunningham 1999).

However, during the 1980s and 1990s, the steady situation changed as digital-recording technologies dramatically lowered the costs of tools and equipment for music-recording. Expensive mixing consoles, tape recorders and other tools required for analogue recording were replaced by digital equivalents which could be bought for a fraction of the cost of their analogue ancestors. This development has continued and, these days, most of the tools required to produce a professional recording are software-based and can fit into ordinary laptop computers. As a consequence, most artists and musicians can afford to create their own complete and professional recording studio in their living room. This new competition from small digital studios has made life difficult for many traditional studios, and even legendary recording studios like The Hit Factory in New York City have been forced out of business (Bukowsky & Connor 2005). However, there seems still to be a demand for some studio services. One example of a studio that has been able to enter the digital music business successfully is the renowned Abbey Road Studios in London, UK. A combination of skilled engineers, first-rate facilities and a decent history has enabled Abbey Road Studios to remain relevant for recording not only large classical music orchestras, but also smaller popular music projects. A completely different studio strategy is to focus less on tools and facilities and more on providing a unique environment to stimulate the artists' creativity. One rather unorthodox studio that has followed this path is Silence Studio in Koppom (pop. 633), Sweden – far away from every global music metropolis. Silence competes with urban studios by being as different from them as possible. As suggested by the name, the studio location allows artists to be immersed in the light, sounds and ambience of the peaceful Nordic natural environment and thereby to reach entirely new creative spheres. One interesting question raised by phenomena such as Silence is whether digital technologies may reduce the importance of being close to music business decision-makers in New York, Los Angeles and London – a question which will be explored in the next section.

Music production and geography
When the music business is in the Cloud, the production of music is almost entirely disconnected from the physical geography. Above, I discussed how the development of new tools for music-recording has driven major recording studios out of business. Popular-music producers no longer have to pay expensive rents to get access to recording facilities, but are able to make high-quality recordings in their own homes with the help of a laptop computer and a couple of decent condenser microphones. In addition, the Internet makes it possible for the artists, musicians and technicians working together on a recording to be located in entirely different locations around the world. For instance, some of the instrumental music might be recorded in Berlin; the recording is then sent to New Delhi, where a talented sitar player adds a solo to the track; finally, the mastering is made in a studio in São Paulo, Brazil.

Based on this reasoning, one might assume that someone who wants a career in the Cloud-based music business can remain in Snohomish and no longer have to move to New York or Tokyo. However, that is not entirely true. Surely it should be possible to sustain a living as an expert in some area and live geographically disconnected from your fellow co-workers. However, research has shown that geography does matter, and the established geographical nodes in the world of music will most likely continue to play important roles in the global music industrial system of the future.

This kind of research is largely based on Michael Porter's work on cluster dynamics during the 1990s. In a number of significant publications (e.g., 1990, 1991) Porter explained how the success of companies is influenced by geographical conditions. His model summarizes a number of factors that determine whether a certain geographical area is good for business or not. The factors in the model constitute a dynamic system that requires considerable time to develop, but if the circumstances are right, a reinforcing feedback loop can be established which may create considerable competitive advantages. The model has been used by economic geographers in the analysis of national and regional economies. It has also been used to analyse the copyright and cultural industries linked to such regions. Hallencreutz and Power have both been influenced by Porter's thinking about regions as dynamic systems and have applied the model to the Nordic music industries (Hallencreutz 2002; Power 2003) and to Swedish copyright industries in general (Power 2002).

This body of research is able to explain how clusters such as Kingston, Jamaica, or Stockholm, Sweden, have been established. They show that physical proximity remains important even though the recording of music may be more or less disconnected from the geography. One explanation for the lingering importance of physical space in the music business is, of course, that recording is merely one part of the overall musical experience. Live music is perhaps even more important to the growth and sustainment of a musical cluster than recorded music, and live music remains as a non-digitizable real-world phenomenon. In addition, many other factors of the music industrial cluster remain linked to the physical world. Music is an inherently communal experience, not only on stage, but also during practising and learning. In order to grow as a musician, it is necessary to meet, play and interact with other musicians, something that preferably occurs in real life.

Talent development

The changed nature of the music producer's profession along with the change in the structure of the music production system are important aspects of making music in the Cloud. The new recording technologies and practices have led to the collapse of the overall costs of making a recording. However, in a world where information is abundant and attention is scarce, the costs of getting that attention have moved in the opposite direction. The music firm's marketing budget for an album project is usually set as a percentage of expected sales. Previously, this percentage hovered around 10 per cent, but changes in the media environment have forced many music firms to let their marketing budgets climb closer to 20 per cent. A marketing director at a major label explains the thinking behind traditional television advertising: 'We have accustomed the consumer to music adverts which has created a situation where more TV spots are required to get the consumer to the record store. Today you need maybe five to ten spots when it previously was enough with less than five.'

However, the actual size of the marketing budgets exhibits an interesting dynamic as a result of its dependence on album sales. When, after the increases in absolute numbers during the 1990s, sales of recorded music plummeted during the early 2000s, marketing budgets shrank at the same time. This change is especially visible in relation to music-video production. The use of moving images to promote music can be traced back to the 1960s (Bob Dylan, The Monkees, The Beatles, et al.) and the 1970s (David Bowie, ABBA, Queen, et al.) but the definitive milestone is the launch of MTV in the US on 1 August 1981 (Denisoff 1988:37). MTV established a new platform for music promotion and spurred the music firms' marketing departments to spend a growing portion of their marketing budgets on the production of promotional videos. This portion expanded because of the assumption that, in order to reach the audience, the video had to beat the extravagance of the competition. This established a reinforcing feedback process which rapidly accelerated music-video production costs, and eventually peaked in 1995 with Michael and Janet Jackson's *Scream*, directed by Mark Romanek, and often cited as the most expensive music video ever made. Now, as a result of the reduced sales of recorded music, music-video production budgets have been considerably reduced, and, also, fewer songs are supported by a promotional video. A former product manager at a major label explains:

> When I started in the music business . . . I had in the beginning I would say for an average music video up to €150,000. When I left [a multinational music firm] in 2003 I had something like a rule that said €50,000 maximum . . . You could feel that the budgets definitely had been reduced . . . we had to get the same media awareness and same media volume for less budget . . . we just didn't have the budgets to work with artists that weren't priority artists, key artists [that] I was hoping to exploit in other territories.

The pattern of behaviour created by the music firms' promotional strategies can be summarized as follows: the transformation of the media environment initially forced music firms to increase their marketing effort and budgets to uphold their media presence. At first, the audience–media engine continued to run fairly well, but as the media environment continued to evolve, music firms were eventually unable to follow suit just by continuously increasing their marketing effort. Consequently, they put on the brakes and, once more, revised their strategies. This time, marketing effort was reduced, but the marketing resources were not evenly distributed across the entire artist roster. The firms' marketing efforts were instead focused on a limited set of prioritized artists, based on the understanding that this was a necessary condition for being heard through the media noise. If marketing costs were to be recouped, prioritized artists had to attract a wide audience appeal. Consequently, artists in the major music firm's roster who could attract only a narrow audience appeal were often less fortunate when competing for the firm's attention and resources.

As fewer artists in the roster gain access to marketing support, it makes no sense for the music firms to hold on to the less successful artists. An A&R agent at a major describes his view on the change: 'Seven years ago I would have hundreds of artists that I wasn't able to give 100 per cent . . . but now when I have reduced the number of artists in the roster, I feel that I am able to pay more attention to every single artist.'

During the emergence of the new music economy, record labels' artist rosters have been significantly reduced. Artists with a broad audience appeal have been prioritized over artists with niche appeal since those in the former category are more likely to recoup the firm's investment in production and marketing. EMI explained its version of this strategy in a press release in March 2004: 'EMI is reducing its global roster by approximately 20 per cent, affecting largely niche and under-performing artists. The roster is being rebalanced to focus resources and efforts more effectively on the artists who have the greatest potential on both a global and local level' (EMI 2004). Following the same reasoning, music firms have grown less patient with their artists. Artists have to be continuously profitable, otherwise they will be dropped from the roster. One classic example of an artist who was unable to create continuously profitable albums is the R&B singer Mariah Carey. During 2001 Carey was signed to EMI, but when her album *Glitter* 'only' sold about 500,000 units, the label decided to terminate its contract with the artist (EMI 2002).

The increased pressure affects the labels' relationships not only with seasoned artists, but also with less experienced talents. Previously, a new artist signed to a major record label was able to learn and evolve during at least two full-length albums. Now, the demands have changed quite considerably. The old adage 'you are only as good as your last recording' has never been more true than today. The A&R agent quoted above reflects on the situation:

> The executives I play our music for . . . when I bring in something that I love . . . they just ask 'where is the hit, where is the single?', they don't want to hear 'this is a great act, let's put them on the road for two years and see what happens', they want to hear which is the radio song and what is the immediate plan to gain them some audience . . . it used to be . . . you can build an artist's career, you might have three albums with that one artist . . . if the first album is not successful you have the second album and the third album . . . now if the first album is not successful, the artist is probably going to be dropped. You have fewer chances with your artist to make it and to become successful . . . it's got to be now . . . everything is very immediate.

While it may be regrettable that so many major artists are now without contracts, it is even more frightening that the major music firms seem no longer to be interested in developing new talent. As an executive explained to us regarding the chances of a new artist remaining on the label: 'One shot and that's it, there are no second chances in this business anymore.' Another informant continued: 'We are signing less number of acts per year, than I probably was, because I don't have the same amount of money as I used to . . . We definitely look for artists that have built up their fan base already and have experience, because first and foremost, you get better with every show . . . yes I definitely want more seasoned road warriors to say the least.'

This change of policy could be described as one whereby the record labels outsource the talent development activity completely. As I noted earlier, for a number of years, smaller independent record labels have been acting as the research and development departments of the music industry (see, e.g., Wallis 1995). Smaller labels have often developed new artists or genres which, when they have reached commercial success, have been acquired by a major. Either the major has acquired the independent label in full, or it has bought out a specific artist in the indie label's roster. This routine has been developed further by majors in the shape of 'upstream deals' signed with the independent labels. An A&R director at a New York-based music publisher commented:

> [The labels] turn to not wanting to do any of the artist develop-
> ment themselves . . . labels are now signing production deals
> with producers and independent labels . . . every label wants
> to do what they call upstream deals . . . where they sign an
> independent label and if it is a rock band they'll let it go in this
> little indie label first . . . the indie label develops it . . . if it sells
> 50,000 or 100,000 units it gets upstreamed to the major . . .
> and that is how a lot of different artists are working these days
> . . . they don't want to spend the money on studio time as they
> used to . . . they don't want to give advances to producers just
> to develop an artist even when they need to grow . . . maybe on
> their second record . . . the labels are not taking those chances
> anymore.

The reasoning in this section shows how the major labels are affected by the new music economy. I have shown that, as costs of marketing climb, labels retreat from the most important components of music business – signing and developing new talents.

The artist as a brand

One way of dealing with the rising costs of attracting and keeping audience attention in the new music economy is to treat artists and bands like brands (see, e.g., Kapferer 2004). It is very costly to establish a new brand. First, the audience has to learn about the existence of the brand; then it has to attach the right values to the brand in question. These processes are usually both expensive and difficult, regardless of industry or product.

It is possible to look at music firms' reluctance to sign new and unproven talents from a brand-management perspective. Basically, since it is costly to develop new brands, it makes sense, from a brand-management perspective, to invest in already established brands, or to build low-risk brands that are able to survive for decades. I shall look into two manifestations of these strategies next.

Table 4.1 The average age of top-10 global superstars	
Period	*Average age*
1989–91	36 yrs
1995–97	42 yrs
2001–03	45 yrs
2004–07	48 yrs
2008–10	44 yrs

Ageing superstars

One way to illustrate the reluctance of music firms to invest in new and unproven talent may be to look at how the age of the highest-earning artists during a given year has changed over the decades. An analysis based on data published in *Forbes, Rolling Stone* and *Billboard* show that, in 1990, the average age of the top-10 global superstars was 36; about two decades later, this had increased to 44 (see Table 4.1).

One explanation for this development might be that music companies simply do not invest enough in new talent to feed the superstar system. However, there could of course be other explanations for the trend. The consumers, the rockers of the 1960s, are growing old alongside their lifelong idols. Not only do these consumers have conservative and unchanging tastes in music, they also have quite a lot of money that they are willing to spend on music. In combination with the fact that adolescents spend less and less money on recorded music, it is possible to conclude that music is being transformed from a pubertal to a geriatric pursuit.

A somewhat morbid extension of the trend of the ageing superstar is that some of the most profitable music brands are related to artists who have actually passed away. The *Forbes* (2011) annual list of the 15 top-earning dead celebrities showed that they grossed a combined $366 million during 2011. Dead songwriters who owned their own catalogue make up a majority of the list, since their estates continue to earn royalties after their death. Elvis Presley has been the highest earning dead celebrity for many years, but since Michael Jackson passed away in 2009, the King of Rock 'n' Roll, whose estate generated $55 million in 2011, has been surpassed by the King of Pop, whose estate earned $170 million during the same period. Besides music-licensing royalties, these revenues are generated by merchandising, theme park entry fees, etc. During recent years, the Canadian entertainment company Cirque de Soleil has risen as a major revenue generator. Cirque de Soleil has produced numerous shows based on works of well-established global music brands, including Las Vegas residencies such as *Viva Elvis* and world-touring shows such as *Michael Jackson: The Immortal World Tour*. The latter production has the prospects of generating more touring revenues for Michael Jackson in his death than when he was alive (*Forbes* 2011).

Manufactured music brands
The second brand-management strategy commonly used in the music industry is to create brands that are unconnected to a flesh-and-blood artist. Examples include connection to a media brand (e.g., a videogame, a radio station, a film or a TV series), a genre (e.g., jazz, garage rock, opera or reggaeton), a certain activity or mood (e.g., relaxation, depression, pregnancy or workout), a time period (e.g., hits from the 1980s), a specific season (e.g., Christmas songs or summer songs), a specific record label (e.g., Sun Records, Motown Records) or simply a collection of recent hits.

There are at least two parties involved in these kinds of projects: the owner of the brand and the owner of the musical content. The rationale behind these projects differs between brand-owner and content-owner. The brand-owner does not necessarily have to be part of the music industry, but might be any kind of consumer-oriented firm. For instance, the clothing manufacturer Levi Strauss & Co. has released a number of albums that include some of the songs licensed for use in their commercials.

It is very rational from a brand-management perspective to

work with brands such as *Pop Idol* or *High School Musical* rather than with traditional artist brands. 'Human' artist brands are considered to be successful if they are able to create four or five profitable albums during their career. This should be contrasted with 'manufactured' music brands, which, if managed well, can go on forever. For example, the *Now That's What I Call Music* compilation series (owned by the major labels) released 853 collections between 1983 and 2012 in 28 territories around the world (http://www.nowmusic.com). Another similar brand, *Absolute*, released more than 250 albums between 1986 and 2012 in Sweden alone. During 2005, every tenth album sold in Sweden was an *Absolute* album (http://www.absolute.se). This arithmetic shows quite bluntly why it is much more appealing, from a business perspective, to establish such a manufactured music brand compared to a traditional one. In addition, manufactured music brands are in less need of promotion tours and radio airplay, they never get old and never have to spend time on drug rehabilitation programmes (Wikström & Burnett 2009).

Televised talent shows
In relation to the sections on music brands and talent development, it is relevant to point to a media phenomenon that became extremely successful during the first decade of this century, namely televised talent shows. Different franchises have reached different levels of success in different territories, but most of them have originated from the UK. Freemantle Media's *Idol* franchise was created in the UK in 2001 and continues to be one of the most popular shows in the US and in many other territories around the world, even though it was cancelled in 2004 in its home country.[21] In the UK, shows such as *Britain's Got Talent* and *The X Factor* have proved to be more successful. Some of the talents scouted during these shows – for instance, Kelly Clarkson, Chris Daughtry, Susan Boyle, Paul Potts and many others – have subsequently experience strong development in their careers. For instance, Kelly Clarkson (US) was the winner

of the first *American Idol* in 2002. Her five albums released since then have all been commercially viable and the second album received two US Grammy awards. Chris Daughtry, who competed in *American Idol* in 2006, formed a band and released a debut album that reached the top position of *Billboard*'s year-end album chart in 2007. Susan Boyle from Scotland amazed the viewers of *Britain's Got Talent* in 2009, and released an album in November 2009 that during five weeks sold more units worldwide (8.3 million) than any other album during that year (IFPI 2010).

As with most unscripted television shows, series such as *Idol* and *Britain's Got Talent* are not particularly well respected by artists with 'cred' or by the cultural elite (see, e.g., Hansson 2004; *Svenska Dagbladet* 2004). However, even after several seasons, the shows continued to receive high ratings in most territories where they have been licensed and they continue to make good economic sense to the parties involved. Broadcasters are happy, since the format attracts an audience that advertisers are willing to purchase. Music firms are also happy, since they are able to find talented personalities. Most importantly, the audience–media engine is kick-started, since these personalities become well known among the mainstream audience before the actual start of their musical careers.

It is reasonable to expect that media brands not immediately linked to a specific music personality of flesh and blood will become more common in the new music economy. There are already a number of successful brands of this kind – for instance, The Gorillaz and The Pussycat Dolls. The 'members' of the former are computer-animated characters, while members of the latter are merely salaried employees of the record label Interscope and hence are completely interchangeable (*The Irish Times* 2006). According to such music industry logic, the performers may still be the face of a project, but they are no longer the 'stars'. Rather, the star is the producer or perhaps the entire creative team managing and controlling the shape and content of the music brand.

Live music

The music industry over the past century has primarily been dominated by the values and perspectives of record companies. Most other parts of the music industry, including live music, have primarily been considered as means to promote the industry's most important product – i.e., the recording. However, during recent decades, the balance between live music and recorded music has shifted. While sales of recorded music have diminished since the early 2000s, revenues from live music have grown rapidly.

There are at least two explanations for the growth of the live music sector. First, the average price of concert tickets has increased and, second, more artists are giving more concerts, which have caused the number of shows to multiply. Let us look into each of these two observations.

The average price of concert tickets has increased significantly more than the average inflation rate in recent years. It is difficult to explain the increase in ticket prices simply by pointing to increasing production costs. Certainly, the live music industry is one that has relatively slow productivity growth, and in such industries prices relate to the increasing costs, which are expected to grow faster than overall inflation. However, this reasoning is unable to explain the sudden change in the growth rate of concert ticket prices at the end of the 1990s. A more plausible explanation of that pattern is related to the performers and their demand for higher guaranteed payment levels. The performers' push for higher guarantees is understandable in the light of falling revenues from recorded music. By increasing the guarantees and, as a consequence, ticket prices, it is possible at least to some extent to compensate for the reduced income from recorded music.

The loss of revenue from recorded music is also able to explain the increase in the number of events. For obvious reasons, a live music experience is difficult to digitize, and is therefore considerably easier to control compared to those areas of the industry that have been affected more profoundly by digital technologies.

CASE STUDY: PRINCE, *PLANET EARTH*

Bundling strategies have been used in various ways in relation to the music industry, for instance when CDs are distributed as covermounts on magazines. One such project involves the R&B artist Prince's 46th album *Planet Earth*. Three million copies of the album were distributed with the British newspaper *Mail on Sunday* on 15 July 2007. The initiative caused much aggravation among bricks-and-mortar retailers, who called the campaign an insult to those who had supported the artist's career during three decades and who now blamed the artist for devaluing his own music. The project is indeed interesting from a bundling perspective (see pp. 114–16), but it also shows how the sales of recorded music has lost its position as the industry's most important revenue-generator. Giving away the recorded music for free, Prince maximized the reach of his music in order to promote the real revenue generator: a residency at the O2 Arena in London produced by AEG Live and comprising 21 shows in total. With 351,000 tickets sold at £31.21 (a reference to his previous album, which was titled *3121*), the series grossed close to £11 million.

Artists who previously were able to earn their livelihood from recorded music have greater and greater difficulty in sustaining their businesses. As a consequence, more and more artists resort to touring, which has caused the number of yearly concert events to grow.

The changing purpose and position of the live music sector
The increasing revenues from live music in combination with the decreasing revenues from recorded music have changed the purpose and position of live concerts in the music industry. In the good old days, live music and touring were the way to promote an artist and to increase the demand for the artist's recordings. Typically, a record was made and a tour was launched to support the sales of that record. It was of less importance whether or not the tour was profitable, since losses generally could be recouped from record sales. However, since the sales of music have decreased so rapidly, it is no longer possible to allow touring projects to be unprofitable. Most live music projects have

to be considered as stand-alone and able to cover their own costs.

During recent years the relationship between live music and recorded music has been reversed. Now, rather than expecting live music to stimulate sales of recorded music, recorded music is often used to stimulate ticket sales. One example of such a project is Prince's *Planet Earth* project in the UK in 2007, which adhered fully to this logic (see Case study).

As a result of the increased importance of live music, the actors within this industry segment have also become more influential in the general music industry. Live Nation, the global giant of the live music business, launched a new business area in 2007, dubbed Live Nation Artists, with the intention of bringing its live performance artists closer to the firm. The business area provides services such as merchandise development and sales, fan-site operation, rights management, ticketing and recordings. By offering these services, it is possible for Live Nation to push the record label out of the equation and to take advantage of a range of revenue streams generated by the artist that are not only limited to live music.

This kind of model, usually referred to as the 360-degree model, has become a more and more common phenomenon in the music industry. It was initially introduced by record labels such as Sanctuary Records in the UK, with the intention of increasing the label's share of the revenues from merchandising, licensing, touring, etc. One early 360-degree deal which gained much attention at the time was the contract between EMI and Robbie Williams, estimated to be worth £80 million (Gibbons 2002). A consequence of the 360-degree model is that sales of recorded music become merely one in a range of other, sometimes larger, revenue streams. Hence, it is not a given that the main actor of such an agreement has to be a record label; it might as well be concert promoters such as Live Nation or even ordinary private equity firms, such as UK-based The Edge Group or Ingenious Media.

Live Nation's first high-profile deal was presented in 2007

when it was able to convince Madonna to leave Warner Music and to sign a new $120 million contract with Live Nation Artists (Smith 2007). The deal marked a massive shift for Madonna, who had been with Warner almost her entire career, starting in 1983. The contract provided the performer with a mix of cash and stock in exchange for the right to sell three albums, promote concert tours, sell merchandise and license her name for sponsorship deals. Madonna received a signing bonus of about $18 million and an advance of roughly $17 million for each of three albums. Another $50 million was handed out in stock and shares.

Live Nation presented another deal in April 2008, when it succeeded in signing Jay-Z to its growing roster (*New York Times* 2008). The contract amounted to $150 million, one of the richest contracts ever awarded to a musician. This partnership, named Roc Nation, included financing for Jay-Z's own entertainment ventures (a record label, talent/management agency and music-publishing company). Live Nation contributed $5 million a year in overheads over five years, with another $25 million available to finance Jay-Z's acquisitions or investments. Roc Nation split the profits with Live Nation.

On 31 March 2008, it was confirmed that U2 signed a 12-year deal with Live Nation worth an estimated $100 million. The deal included Live Nation controlling the band's merchandise, sponsoring and their official website. Other artists who have signed with Live Nation include Nickelback and Shakira. Mainly a concert promoter, Live Nation 'signs' artists as a 'record label', but predominantly takes on the role of a promoter, rather than 'owner of music'.

Depending on the outcome of these new deals and experiments, the relationship between artist and music company might well never be the same again, thus having tremendous consequences for the future of the entire music industry. The revival of the live music sector is also one of the most important features of the new music economy. One might argue that, as the music firms' ability to control their assets in a digital format diminishes, live music will soon dominate the entire music industry in the same fashion as recorded music has done during more than half a century.

The relationship between the artist and what used to be the record label

The 360-degree model discussed above has gained lots of attention since its inception. Some consider it to be the future of the music industry, while others think it is extremely unwise for – especially younger – artists to put all their eggs in one basket. Proponents of the model are often also positive about seeing the artist as a brand. Based on that thinking, investments in a particular brand – i.e., an artist's career – will increase the equity of the brand, which, in turn, will generate revenues from sponsorships, film acting, merchandise, touring, licensing and, of course, music sales. They argue further that it is reasonable that a record label that builds that brand equity should also get the returns from all revenues, not only from one or a few of them.

From the artist's point of view, there is some attraction in signing a 360-degree contract. Usually these contracts include rather hefty advances, and in addition it is very convenient only to have to deal with one company for all business-related matters. The problem is, however, that artists who sign such a contract may run the risk of losing some of their creative control. In the relationship between artist and record label, there is always a trade-off between business risk and creative control. The 360-degree deal is placed on the very end on a spectrum where the record labels accept most of the business risk, and the artists lose most of their creative control. On this spectrum, there is a variety of different contractual models that differ in terms of the balance between risk and control. I will look at some of these models next.

The contractual structure somewhat 'to the right' of the 360-degree deal is the traditional record label contract. In this structure, the label pays for the recording and handles the manufacturing, distribution, press and promotion. The artist gets an advance payment and a royalty percentage after all those other costs have been repaid. If an album is a commercial failure and is unable to earn back the firm's expenses, no royalties will be paid to the artist. Since most album projects are unprofitable, it is not uncommon that artists live in constant debt to their record label, and if they hit a dry spell they can go broke.

In this type of contract, the label owns the copyright of the recording forever and ultimately decides if and how recordings should be distributed and promoted. This means that if an artist has made a recording which does not fit with the label's understanding of what kind of music is marketable – if label executives 'don't hear a single' (cf. the quotation on p. 133) – the recording might never be released.

One of the strongest objections to the traditional record label contract is the transfer of ownership of the copyrights from the artist to the record label. The licence deal is similar to the standard deal, except in this case the artist retains the copyrights and ownership of the master recording. The right to exploit that property is granted to a label for a limited period of time – usually seven years. After that, the rights to license to TV shows, commercials and the like revert to the artist. If a band has made a record itself and doesn't need creative or financial help, this model is often optimal. It allows for more creative freedom, since there is less interference from the record company executives. The downside is that, because the label does not own the master recording, it may invest less in making the release a success.

As the music industry evolves, the licence is becoming more common. There are several drivers behind this trend. First, the growing importance of copyrights and licensing has made artists increasingly aware of the importance of retaining the rights to their recordings. Second, in the old days, burgeoning artists tried to convince A&R agents by sending them relatively basic recordings of their creative ideas; today's artists can finance their own recordings, and are able to send full-fledged recordings of professional quality to the record labels. Correspondingly, as has been discussed above, record labels are unwilling to invest in unproven artists. In a licensing deal, the record label reduces its risk since it can make a decision regarding a specific recording without having invested anything in advances or recording costs. If the label likes the recording, it will sign the contract for that particular recording, pay an advance to the artist and begin its promotion and distribution activities. The artist is then free to pursue his or her luck with other labels.

There are several variations of the licensing deal. One involves changing the balance between the advances and the royalties paid by the label to the artist. This balance is not related to creative control, but only to how the business risk is shared between label and artist. Another variation might concern what kind of services the record label should perform, whether manufacturing the physical product, physical distribution, online distribution, promotion, etc.

As the new music economy has evolved, contracts whereby the artist retains more of the control and the role of the record label is reduced become more and more common. A question soon arises: when does the record label cease to be a record label? In the old days, the primary role of the record label was to finance the recording and to manufacture, distribute and promote the disk. In the new music economy, artists are able to control all these activities themselves. They are able to make the recording in their own studio; they can hire specific consultants and service companies which are happy to offer services such as marketing communication, online distribution, and so on. There is no place for the record label in the new music economy. Some services are required, and there will certainly be a demand from artists for financing, distribution services, promotion services, tour production, and so on, and perhaps these services will be provided by companies that previously referred to themselves as record labels, but the relationship between these entities and the artists will almost certainly never be like the twentieth-century record contract.

During most of the twentieth century, the record labels more or less ran the music industry. They were in power, they controlled

CASE STUDY: ROBYN CARLSSON

The career of the Swedish pop act Robyn Carlsson is a very telling story about the old and the new music economy.

1995	At the age of 16 Robyn Carlsson releases her own songs 'You've Got That Something' and the breakthrough single 'Do You Really Want Me'. The singles are followed by the debut album *Robyn Is Here* produced by Cheiron's Max Martin and Denniz Pop.
1997	The singles 'Do You Know (What It Takes)' and 'Show Me Love' are released in the US and reach the *Billboard* top 10.
1999	The album *My Truth* is released in Europe and the single 'Electric' is on heavy rotation. In the US, the BMG label RCA refuses to release the album unless Robyn makes some of the songs more radio-friendly. She refuses and the record is never released in the US.
2002	The third album, *Don't Stop the Music*, is released by BMG. Because of continued problems with the record label, it is only released in Sweden.
2004	Robyn makes a recording of the song 'Who's That Girl'. Again, the record label refuses to release the song, and instead releases 'Robyn's Best' in the US.
2005	After all the problems with her business partner BMG, she is able to end the contract and start her own company, Konichiwa Records. Later that year, she records the album *Robyn* together with producers Klas Åhlund and Alexander Kronlund. Initially, Konichiwa has considerable problems with getting the CD out in retail stores because the majors were very hesitant to include the product in their distribution machinery.
2006	Robyn wins several Swedish Grammy Awards, among others for Best Album, Best Female Artist and Best Composer (together with Klas Åhlund).
2007	*Robyn* is released in the UK and is well received by critics and fans.
2008	The album is released in the US. Robyn receives rave reviews and appears on the David Letterman show. The single 'With Every Heartbeat' reaches the number one spot on the official UK chart and she has a sold-out tour in the UK. Robyn supports Madonna on her European 'Sticky & Sweet' tour.
2009	Robyn starts working on the *Body Talk* recording project together with Klas Åhlund. The songs are released as three

albums in June, September and November the following year. The project is seen as an attempt to break up the traditional album structure. *Body Talk* was considered by Entertainment Weekly, MTV and *Billboard* to be the third-best album released during 2010.

Peter Swartling, Robyn's first producer from 1993, comments on her future career: 'Robyn is the ultimate artist but her future success has nothing to do with her talent and artistry. If it only would depend on that there would be no limit to how big she could get. Now it is all about how she is able to manage her resources and her distribution channels . . . Today it is much more difficult to release an artist compared to 4–5 years ago, and it depends more than ever on external conditions.'

Sources: Yeaman 2008; Madonna.com 2008; *McLean* 2010.

the distribution resources, they retained the rights to the intellectual properties, and so on. Throughout this book, I have shown how revenues from recorded music have diminished, while revenues from the other two industry sectors – music-licensing and live music – have increased. I have also shown how the services offered by record labels either are no longer in demand or are offered by more agile competitors.

In the new music economy, the record label is no longer in the driver's seat; it is the artist, or the artist/manager, who is. In the new music economy, the artist's role as an (involuntary) entrepreneur is strengthened. Rather than being contracted by a record company to perform certain services, the artist sets up a limited company and secures the necessary funding as he or she sees fit. As in any limited company, funding may be in the shape of equity or liabilities; it may be from venture capitalists, from banks or from the stock market. The value of the company is raised through the accumulation of revenues from various activities and the intellectual assets developed by the artist. Most likely, expenses also have to be paid for services such as distribution, promotion, etc. Of course, these kinds of companies existed also in the old music economy, but they are now becoming increasingly common.

I started out this book by looking at the case of Trent Reznor and Nine Inch Nails. Reznor is one of the many artists to follow this model. Radiohead (see the Case study on p. 113) is another one, and so is the Swedish pop act Robyn (see Case study on p. 146), with her label Konichiwa Records. There are of course variations within the scope of this basic structure, ranging from the massive ventures such as Live Nation Artists, via mid-sized management firms such as ie:music[22] in London, to single-artist endeavours such as Robyn's Konichiwa Records in Stockholm.

This is a new music-making structure, which differs radically from the old music economy. If the transformation continues, it might considerably lower the concentration of the production of music, which should call for an increase in the diversity of the music that is produced (e.g., Dowd 2000; 2004).

This chapter has explored how professional music-making is transformed. I have looked at how the professions and practices within the production of music have changed, discussed how the development of new talents has been affected by the new business conditions, and explored how artists' careers increasingly are modelled as a matter of brand management. I continued with the development within the live music sector and the evolving relationship between the artist and its business partners. I discussed the 360-degree model, but also other structures for the agreements between artists and what formerly used to be the record label. Building on this analysis, I envisioned a future where the creative artists and their managers take the leading role in the industry, which might lead to increased cultural diversity.

The next chapter will continue the analysis of music-making, but I will leave the realm of the so-called professionals, and move on to the amateurs.

5

The Social and Creative Music Fan

Music plays an important role in many people's lives. It can wake you up in the morning and it can slow you down after work. It can get you in the mood for love and it can comfort your broken heart. It can connect you to your peers and separate you from conventions and older generations. However, there are some people who want to do more than simply listen to the music. They want to sing along or even play their own versions of their favourite songs; they want to share their feelings and musical experiences with their peers and the world; and they want to learn about every detail of the life of the celebrities. I have previously discussed how improved connectivity and more widely accessible upload capability have lowered the barriers to entering the media outlet market (see p. 90). However, in the new music economy, these barriers are so low that every amateur musician and ordinary music fan is able to create, remix and publish music online.

The phenomenon whereby the audience not only passively consumes culture but also contributes in the production of that culture is often referred to as participatory culture (Jenkins 2006). Participatory culture is not at all restricted to music but can be seen in other cultural spheres such as the film, videogame or book arenas. Thousands of blogs discuss the latest developments of the *Lord of the Rings* or the *Star Wars* franchises. Teenagers write and publish their own stories (i.e., fan fiction) based on Harry Potter or Buffy the Vampire Slayer, thereby taking the characters into new, and at times controversial, territories. Music fans make their own music videos to their favourite song to express how the song makes them feel. While participatory culture is a trend pushed from the consumers' desire to be creative and social, there is another driving force towards the increased involvement of consumers in the provisioning and development of services. Providers of services such as banking, travel, healthcare, etc., increasingly try to involve the consumer in their value-creation processes. Consumers are allowed direct access to the banking system to do stock trading, make money transfers or make invoice payments themselves. Online questionnaires allow patients to begin a process of self-diagnosis before meeting a doctor in the flesh. Again, it is the digital technologies that are facilitating this trend, and the motivation from the service providers' point of view is, of course, to lower their costs.

This chapter will explore the consumption of music, the role of the music fan and the relationship between the fan and the celebrity in the new music economy. I shall look at different parts of the value-creation process of the music business and how consumers are involved in the different phases. I also look at how some fans help in the promotion of their favourite artists. I start out with the last phase of the value chain: distribution.

Friendly sharing?

In chapter 3, I discussed connectivity–control aspects of the new music economy, and how rights holders have lost the ability to control the distribution of their intellectual properties. Perhaps the single most important technological concept that has pushed that irreversible process forward is peer-to-peer (P2P) networking. P2P networking is basically a principle for communicating and sharing resources in a computer network. It differs from the traditional computer network topology known as 'client–server networking', in which a single powerful computer serves the requests of a large number of less powerful computers, or clients. In such a network, communication between two clients has to pass through the server, which makes it relatively easy to monitor and control. If, for instance, a client in the client–server network distributes MP3 files without the rights holder's authorization, it is easy to locate that client and charge its owner with copyright infringement. In a true P2P network there exists no central server, and communication takes place directly between the computers connected to the network. In this kind of situation, communication is much more difficult to police. In modern P2P networks, a single music file (or any kind of digital information) is split up into several pieces and stored in a large number of computers, which makes it even harder to determine who is responsible for the distribution of that particular file.

It should be noted that P2P networking as such is neither suspicious nor illegal. P2P concepts have been discussed within the Internet research community since 1969, when Steve Crocker brought the issue to the table (Crocker 1969). Several P2P networks have been launched since – for instance, UseNet in 1979 and FidoNet in 1984. Since mainstream personal computers have become ever more prevalent and the bandwidth by which these computers are connected to the Internet has grown, P2P has become an increasingly useful model for Internet-based collaboration and networking. Today, P2P networking is used in several entirely legal applications – primarily for media distribution, but also for other purposes such as Internet telephony (Oram 2001).

Although P2P networking has a long history and many legitimate uses, when in 1999 it reached the general public in the shape of the Napster software, it became forever linked to the illegal distribution of recorded music (Alderman 2001). The Napster software spread quickly among Internet users and grew to giant proportions. This development did not go unnoticed by the major record labels, which brought the Napster creator Shawn Fanning to trial, where he was issued with a cease-and-desist order. Fanning eventually followed that order, but once the P2P concept was known among the general public, other more sophisticated technologies soon followed.

File-sharing networks as Cloud-based music libraries
There has been, and still is, a relatively polarized debate over whether the copyright infringements enabled by P2P networking and other similar technologies caused the downturn of the recorded music industry. Most rights holders, and the majority of the 'establishment', argue that digital technologies, such as P2P networking, enable consumers to acquire music without the owners' consent and without paying for the use of the products. These arguments focus on the fundamental aspects of property law and property owners' rights to decide how their assets should be exploited and used. According to this reasoning, illegal file-sharing has enabled consumers to reduce their purchases of recorded music through legitimate channels and to turn to free but illegal methods of acquiring music.

The second argument is primarily held by an exotic mix of apolitical Internet techies, anarchists and radical liberals. According to their reasoning, music firms actually benefit from the audience's increased access to musical content, which has facilitated audience action (cf. the audience–media engine) and enabled more people to discover music and broaden their musical experience – all of which is beneficial to the entire music industry. Based on this logic, the appropriate action by the music industry would be to support the uncontrolled circulation of copyrighted material on the Internet, rather than to try to wipe it out.

Several scholars and research firms have contributed to the debate. Research on US consumers shows a negative relationship between files downloaded and CDs purchased (Edison Media Research 2003; Ipsos-Reid 2002). Research made on European consumers also shows that the impact of online piracy on sales is negative. Forrester Research (2003) concluded that more than 40 per cent of frequent 'downloaders' buy less music now than they did before they began downloading. Indeed, 2 per cent of the 'downloaders' say they bought more CDs after they started downloading, but that is in no way able to balance the loss. Enders Analysis (2003) joins the choir by stating that online piracy 'cost about 35–40 per cent of the reduction in the size of the global music market'.

The conclusion from these research reports indicates that there are other factors influencing sales of recorded music besides the emergence of specific Internet technologies. This conclusion is supported by several scholars – for instance Liebowitz (2002a; 2002b), who points to the general state of the economy, and Wikström (2005), who points to changes among the broadcast media and music firms' revised A&R strategies. Some scholars go as far as to argue that the effect of Internet technologies on CD sales 'is statistically indistinguishable from zero' (Oberholzer & Strumpf 2005).

We will probably never be able to determine the detailed impact of illegal file-sharing on the sales of recorded music. The consumer behaviour dynamics are simply too complex. However, it is vital to recognize that P2P file-sharing is an important Cloud-based music service, perhaps the most important one, and certainly the most widely used. As has already been mentioned, for every track legally purchased online, 20 tracks are downloaded from P2P networks (IFPI 2008). But it is important not to make the same mistake as many record labels when comparing these two ways of acquiring music. One track downloaded from a P2P network does not necessarily correspond to one track purchased at a single-song download service. Rather, the relation between P2P networks and single-song download services (or CDs for that matter) should be compared to the relationship between libraries and bookstores. Consumers who download from P2P networks behave and think very differently from those who interact with single-song download retailers. At the single-song-download retailer, consumers are quite sure which songs they like or dislike before they actually make the purchase. At P2P networks, consumers may download the entire Elvis Presley catalogue out of curiosity after having heard 'Jailhouse Rock'. They may choose to download songs they have already purchased simply because they are using their laptop computer, and not the living-room computer where those songs are stored. P2P file-sharing networks are Cloud-based music libraries rather than head-on competitors to single-song-download services. It is important to note that I am not arguing that there is no impact from the use of online piracy on legitimate music sales. The bulk of the reports presented in recent years increasingly supports the case that online piracy in aggregate has a negative effect on the sales of recorded music. This position has been held by many music firms from the very beginning, and they have spent considerable resources trying to minimize consumers' unsanctioned file-sharing activities and to recapture control of music distribution from the hands of the audience.

Music firms' response to online piracy
Music firms, like most other rights holders, try to protect the value of their assets. The intellectual property portfolio often constitutes a major part of the music firm's balance sheet, and if something or someone is threatening to diminish the value of the firm's assets, it is the duty of the management to act. It is not the first time the music industry has been concerned about copyright infringement and the potential loss of distribution control. When compact cassette technology was developed, it also incited a creative and social music listening culture with phenomena such as dubbing, bootlegging and mixtaping.[23] A whole range of new audience actions was opened up to the public. However, it was difficult to collect immediate revenues from the audience's new actions. The industry decided to respond by launching information campaigns such as IFPI's legendary 'Home taping is killing music – and it's illegal' initiative during the 1980s. The industry also successfully lobbied against governments in order to introduce a levy on cassette recorders and on blank, recordable cassettes. The levy would compensate copyright owners for the illegal use (e.g., dubbing) of the cassette technology. It should be noted that in some nations, for instance in the UK, the trade organizations did not want the blank cassette levy. They argued that, by introducing such a mechanism, they were

indirectly accepting copyright infringements, such as dubbing and bootlegging.

The response from the industry during this period has many parallels to how it reacted to the impact from digital technologies. The strategic actions within this area have been documented by many scholars (see, e.g., Barfe 2004; Freedman 2003; Imfeld 2004).

Several initiatives have been aimed directly at the consumers. First, a number of information campaigns have been launched by various trade bodies. The purpose of these initiatives has been to influence the understanding and the attitudes, primarily among young people, about copyright-related issues. The international trade body of the recording industry, IFPI, runs the 'Pro Music' campaign in several music markets.[24] Its US affiliate RIAA has a similar initiative aimed at the domestic market called 'Music United',[25] and music publishers in the UK operate the 'Respect the value of music' campaign, via the trade organization British Music Rights (BMR).

Second, an initiative primarily launched by trade organizations representing record labels consists of lawsuits filed against organizations and individuals who violate copyright legislation. These lawsuits have been especially prevalent in the US market, where 18,000 cases have been filed by the RIAA during recent years. Trade organizations in Europe have been less aggressive and have only filed approximately 5,500 lawsuits in 18 countries (Millard 2006).

Third, the music recording industry has supported the development of various techniques to restrict and control the copying of music. These technologies have often failed, since some have made listening to CDs via certain players difficult, and others have seriously threatened the consumer's personal integrity (Borland 2005). In spite of all these and other similar initiatives intended to regain control and to stop illegal file-sharing, the P2P networks still elude the threats from the copyright industries. Since illegal file-sharing tries to stay under the radar as much as it can, it is, for obvious reasons, rather difficult to get reliable data on the development of file-sharing activities. Figure 5.1 shows a rather dated graph that ends in January 2006, which indicates how the number of simultaneous users of P2P network services has developed. This graph does not, however, include one of the most common P2P network protocols, BitTorrent. Other investigations into the development of file-sharing and P2P network usage (e.g., Sandvine 2012; BitTorrent 2012) suggest that in 2012 there were more than a quarter of a billion monthly active BitTorrent users worldwide and that BitTorrent traffic continues to grow in absolute numbers, although its share of total Internet traffic is diminishing due to the growth of legitimate entertainment streaming services such as Netflix, Hulu, etc.

Perhaps the single most enduring effect of the rights holders' attempts to limit online piracy has been a negative impact on the reputation of the music industry. Entertainment industries, including the music industry, have long been suffering from a rather bad reputation. Negus recognizes this by referring to music companies (in somewhat ironic terms) as 'commercial corrupters and manipulators' (1996: 46). Other texts have used Hunter Thompson's provocative description of the television business to describe the music industry: 'Mainly we are dealing with a profoundly degenerate world, a living web of foulness, greed and treachery' (1988: 43).

Music industry decision-makers are well aware of the damage that their efforts to regain control of distribution has caused to their already injured reputation. Nevertheless, they see no other option but to do everything possible in order to sustain the value of their intellectual properties: 'It just looks like we are anti every new technology that comes around . . . but that's not true really, I mean sometimes it is true but that is for good reason, for good business reason. That's hard to get across to the media or the public' (trade organization representative).

Another kind of strategic initiative that has proved more effective has been to lobby multilateral organizations and governments to revise copyright treaties and legislations. In 1996, the 183 member states of the World Intellectual Property

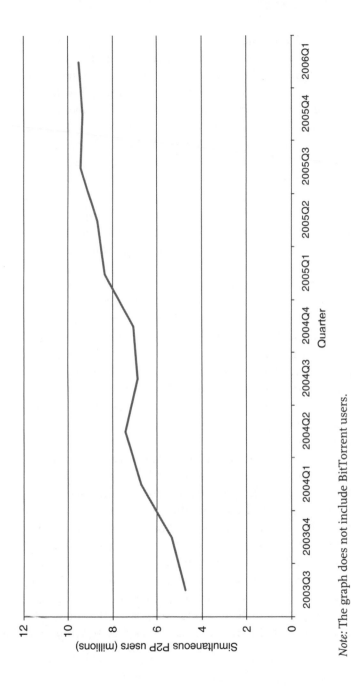

Note: The graph does not include BitTorrent users.

Figure 5.1 The number of simultaneous P2P users worldwide continues to grow

Source: BigChampagne Media Measurement (http://www.bigchampagne.com)

Organization (WIPO) adopted the WIPO Copyright Treaty. The aim was to adapt the copyright treaty to the development of digital information and communication technologies. The treaty ensured, among other things, that computer software was protected by the copyright legislation in the member states. It has, since 1996, slowly been implemented: in the US as the Digital Millennium Copyright Act (DMCA) in 1998, and in the EU as the European Union Copyright Directive (EUCD) in 2001. Almost all the individual member states of the EU have, since 2001, implemented the EUCD in their national legislations. In the countries where the treaty has been implemented, copyright legislation has generally been tightened and the punishment for infringing and violating the legislation has been increased.

Even though the tightening process that has been going on for more than a decade has been eagerly applauded by the copyright firms, it is not possible to attribute the revised copyright legislation among WIPO member states entirely to copyright industry lobbying. It is also still too early to say what effect so-called 'graduate response' legislation, as implemented in France and the UK, will have on the illegal file-sharing activities.[26] At least so far, the P2P-based file-sharing activity seems to remain relatively strong. If rights holders become even more aggressive and decide to use the legal weaponry they have at their disposal to their full capability, it would have significant and perhaps unexpected consequences for the music industry. Music firms would probably be able to increase their level of control, decrease network connectivity and increase their revenues from various audience actions. However, as the level of control has an inverse relationship with the level of accessibility, the more tightly the content is controlled, the more difficulty consumers will have in accessing and gaining awareness of that content. Following such a path would have a hampering effect on the audience–media engine, which in turn would work against – or maybe even cancel out – any revenue increase caused by the improved control.

The audience as amateur musicians

During the days of analogue media technologies, the ability to create high-quality media artefacts was restricted to those who had access to expensive facilities and tools for professional audio and video production. As discussed in previous chapters, digital technologies have dramatically changed this situation and made it possible for anyone equipped with an ordinary laptop to create and upload sounds and images of at least semi-professional quality.

This development, combined with the audience's improved access to digital sounds and images online, has opened up what is often referred to as a 'remix culture' (e.g., Tapscott & Williams 2006: 137). Remix culture is closely related to Jenkins's participatory culture, but emphasizes the phenomenon of consumers' using bits and pieces of existing popular culture to create new meanings and new artefacts. This kind of cultural recycling is manifested in several ways in the area of music.

One example is what is known as 'plunderphonics', a term coined by the composer and performer John Oswald in 1985 to denote musical works solely made out of samples of existing recordings. Another instance of musical recycling is the 'mash-up', which is a musical work made by remixing instrumental sound from one song with the vocals from another. While the majority of user-generated plunderphonics and mash-ups are most likely to end up as an obscure blog-post, some (almost) professional artists have also picked up the technique and created works that actually have reached a relatively respectable level of recognition. Prank Monkey's *London Booted* from 2004, primarily based on the Clash's *London Calling* from 1979, is one fine example, and Danger Mouse's *Grey Album* from the same year, which combined The Beatles' *The White Album* (1968) with Jay-Z's *The Black Album* (2003) is another. Jay-Z's *The Black Album* is interesting for another reason too, since it includes *a cappella* versions of the tracks, specifically to facilitate new remixes and mash-ups. Perhaps it is not entirely surprising that a hip-hop artist such as Jay-Z would make such a move, since musical recycling as well as sampling are at the core of hip-hop culture. However, it shows how established producers have picked up the concepts of the remix culture.[27]

Another manifestation of remix culture is the creation of fan videos based on a popular song. This phenomenon has gained strong momentum, together with YouTube's positioning as the leading website for all kinds of user-generated videos. There are many different kinds of fan videos: some are slideshows intended to illustrate a user's sincere interpretation of a song and others are homemade videos of a fan impersonating the artist, often with an ironic twist.

Some fan videos are more technically sophisticated, created by editing short clips into a coherent video. The conventions and aesthetics of the videos vary. One important genre is the Anime Music Video (AMV) that is made out of short clips from Japanese Anime movies, where the characters' lip movements are synched with the lyrics of the song. As so often in the pop cultural sphere, conventions, values and fads are shaped through a conversation between a creative audience and the professional pop cultural creators. In the case of AMVs, the team behind Britney Spears chose to use Anime aesthetics when creating her 2008 music video 'Break the Ice'. However, some of her fans did not approve of the video, which did not follow the traditional Britney Spears video format. In response, Philip Campbell Jr., a Britney fan from Snohomish in the US, decided to make his own version of the 'Break the Ice' video, based on clips from Spears's older music videos and stage performances. In June 2008, the official video had more than 8 million views on YouTube, while Campbell's version received more than 2 million views, which is a fairly impressive number for a court reporter from Snohomish.

Another interesting genre is the Slash music video, which normally tells a homoerotic story in which characters from one narrative are given new meanings by combining the right sounds with the right images. For some reason it has become very popular to use the *Star Trek* characters Mr Spock and Captain Kirk as the basis for such Slash music videos. Fans have created numerous videos around these characters, based on songs such as Justin Timberlake's 'SexyBack', Nine Inch Nails' 'Closer' and Divinyls' 'I Touch Myself'. While irony is an important ingredient in many fan videos, several of them are made with what at least seems to be complete sincerity and true appreciation of the artist. The fan-made 'Break the Ice' video mentioned above probably belongs to that category, together with many other fan-made videos of songs in almost every thinkable musical genre.

The amount of user-generated online content is growing at a staggering rate, and the examples above are only a few samples taken from a wide range of works generated by creative fans. During the analogue age, there were many hurdles to be overcome before a writer, composer, artist – or anybody else for that matter – could get their works known to the world. The very process of getting work published was defining for many such professions; for instance, you became a writer if you had a book accepted by a publisher. In the digital age, anyone can get published, so anyone can be a writer. There are of course still many hurdles to be overcome before the work of an artist or writer actually reaches the audience's awareness zone, but at least today both the distribution and the production bottlenecks have almost entirely gone. Every day, 175,000 new weblogs are launched, and 1.6 million new posts are published. YouTube, the largest web community for user-generated videos, claims that 10 hours of video content is uploaded to their service every minute.

This development takes us towards an interesting future where the ratio between the amount of professionally generated content and the amount of user-generated content available online is asymptotically approaching zero. In other words, almost all content available online is user-generated and only a small fraction is created by those people who actually write texts, make movies or sing songs professionally. In a world coloured by the virtues of the remix culture, it will become virtually impossible to charge users for simple access to content (cf. the discussion in chapter 3). It is interesting to speculate how such a development will affect the professional production of popular culture. It will probably be increasingly difficult to create profitable entertainment projects such as full-length motion pictures or traditional music albums. In order to survive, the producers should, rather, focus on providing tools and building blocks for the users to create their own material. Surely, something similar to the traditional movie or album could also be provided, merely as an example of how the building blocks might be put together, but what is most important is that a service is offered that inspires and stimulates the users' creativity (cf. the Nine Inch Nails case on p. 1). By creating such a service, it would be possible to attract the users' attention for minutes or hours and advertisers could be charged for the immediate access to the users' open minds.

Music promotion goes viral

One of the themes of this book is the music firms' loss of control. Above, I discussed the loss of distribution control, but music firms also have less control over other parts of the music business value chain. One such area is the promotion of music.

One significant trend that has changed the rules of music promotion is the growing importance of Internet-based social network services. An Internet-based social network service allows people who share a common interest of some kind to communicate, cooperate and socialize. The notion of connecting a set of computers in order to facilitate social networking is fundamentally linked with the early development of the Internet during the 1970s. Two pioneering services of very different character are Usenet, launched in 1979, and the Well, launched in 1985.

While these early social network services were primarily focused on discussions about certain topics between people, contemporary social network services support a range of other kinds of communicative actions. Facebook, Twitter, LinkedIn, Instagram, Pinterest and other social network services increasingly take over all aspects that were once associated with the Internet as a whole. Facebook, the leading social network service that claims to have more than a billion users worldwide (October 2012), is a platform where people hang out with their friends and family, keep and display their family photo albums, read their news, play their games and, last but not least, discover new music and tell their friends about the music they love. It is a platform where users are able to perform, create and communicate their identities to the world.

The consumption of stories, music and other cultural artefacts has always been a useful device for communicating an individual's identity. In a world where stories and music are primarily distributed as books, records, tapes and other physical formats, the living-room cabinet – where all these mementos are put on display – serves as an intimate and significant marker of a person's identity. Visiting friends can browse through the collection and draw conclusions about the owner's identity based on the books and the albums that he or she has included in the assortment of 'sacred items' (Giles et al. 2007).

On the other hand, in a world where stories and music are distributed as data files in a data network rather than as discs on a truck, Facebook and other social network services have taken over the traditional role of the living-room bookshelf as the beacon for identity communication (see, e.g., Baym 2010; Mjøs 2012; Suhr 2012). With social media services such as last.fm and Facebook, music listeners are able to broadcast to the world what they are listening to at any given moment. The role of record collections as a manifestation of people's musical identity has been replaced by a steady flow of information about their real-time musical experiences. Listening to music has always been a social activity, but the 'virtualization of the living-room bookshelf' radically transforms the communal aspects of a person's listening experience. Sharing this experience is no longer based on *purchase* decisions made over an extended period of time. Rather, it is based on *listening* decisions made in real time. Second, these listening decisions are shared not only with one's most intimate friends in the sanctity of one's home; they are shared also with one's Facebook friends or perhaps even with the general online public.

Recommendations from trusted friends have a strong influence on our decisions, regardless of whether those decisions concern one's lifestyle or what type of music to listen to. As users of social network services automatically and in real time share information about the music they listen to, so their role as collective tastemakers becomes stronger at the expense of the top-down promotion from record labels and rights holders. So-called word-of-mouth processes are in no way new to the music industry, and there are numerous examples from the old music economy of how artists, using similar procedures, have gained a foothold in a territory or market.

One such example from the analogue age concerns the Swedish pop act Roxette. Roxette was completely unknown in the US until, in 1988, Dean Cushman, an American exchange student from Minneapolis, took a copy of the Roxette album *Look Sharp!* home with him from Sweden. Cushman urged a local Minneapolis radio station, KDWB 101.3 FM, to play the album and, based on positive feedback from callers, the station's programme director copied it and distributed it to other stations. Within weeks, *Look Sharp!* became popular throughout the region and, ultimately, nationwide. On 8 April 1989, the single 'The Look' reached the number one position of *Billboard*'s Hot 100 and eventually Roxette turned out to be one of the most successful Swedish exports since the days of ABBA (see, e.g., *Billboard Magazine* 1989; Thorselius 2003).

Through the growing importance of social networks, these kinds of uncontrolled processes are no longer merely random flukes, but are slowly becoming more or less the norm of music promotion in the digital age. In the new music economy, music firms are increasingly dependent on their fans to create a strong media presence and to promote their music. The clever music firm does not have to shout louder, by increasing its marketing budget, in order to compensate for the raised audience fragmentation – it can promote its artists by supporting fans' desire to express themselves through the music.

The rapid information diffusion processes that take place in a

CASE STUDY: WHEN THE PROMOTION BECOMES THE ART FORM – *YEAR ZERO* BY NINE INCH NAILS

The Los Angeles-based 'industrial rocker' Trent Reznor, a.k.a. Nine Inch Nails, has a very loyal fan base. Reznor's music is violent, dark and dystopian and seems to appeal to a demographic consisting of computer-literate Quake*-playing young men. In 2007, Reznor released a project titled *Year Zero*. From one perspective, *Year Zero* adheres to traditional music promotion logic. A 16-track album was released and supported by a series of promotion activities aimed at Reznor's core audience, the computer-literate young men. However, from another perspective, *Year Zero* should not be considered merely as an album, but as interactive multimedia art, where the album is only one component among many others.

Besides being a concept album, where Reznor paints a dystopian vision of a world to come, *Year Zero* is also a so-called alternate reality game (ARG), which takes place in the physical world as well as online. A narrative is told by releasing subtle clues and puzzles which the players are supposed to discover and solve together. The 3.5 million fans who played *Year Zero* found clues as hidden messages on Nine Inch Nails tour T-shirts, on USB memory sticks that someone had left behind in the bathroom at a concert venue, as cryptic video clips on YouTube, and so on.

It would be close to impossible to create a successful ARG without using the Internet as a platform for communication. To solve a puzzle, fans might have to look for clues on different continents and combine the brains of a computer science graduate and an expert on Sumerian language. The 'hive mind' made up by the Internet-connected Nine Inch Nails fans solved many of these clues relatively quickly and were thereby able to propel the narrative to the next phase.

Year Zero was produced by 42 Entertainment, a company that, to a large extent, has driven the evolution of ARGs as multimedia experiences/promotional tools. 42 Entertainment has previously worked with ARGs, for instance related to the A.I. motion picture, the Halo 2 videogame and Microsoft's Windows Vista.

It is of course naive to deny that one important purpose of an ARG is to increase the sales of a product or improve the recognition and value of a brand. But the ARG also delivers entertainment value that makes it into a fascinating experience by itself. In the music industry in the digital age, it is difficult to say whether the concert is promoting the album or if it is the other way around. The same reasoning is transferable to the relationship between an ARG and an album. Is it really the ARG that is promoting the album or is it perhaps the other way around?

Quake is a first-person-shooter videogame developed by id Software.

friction-free network are extremely difficult to predict and control. Such a system is extremely sensitive to minor changes in its initial conditions, and insignificant events (as in the Roxette story) can lead to radical shifts in the system's behaviour. Often these processes are referred to as 'viral', since there are many similarities to how an airborne viral disease spreads across an area. It is not uncommon for non-commercial user-based content, such as YouTube videos, funny jokes and websites, suddenly to go viral. One of the more extreme examples is probably the video entitled 'Charlie Bit My Finger – Again', about the English brothers Charlie and Harry. The father posted the video on YouTube in May 2007 and, lo and behold, six years later, the 56-second-long video has been viewed more than 500 million times and is one of the most viewed videos on YouTube – ever!

While this may happen once in a while quite unexpectedly, as in the Charlie case or the Roxette case, it is not a viable communication strategy for a profit-maximizing music firm. The question is whether and how music firms are able to mimic the success of the user-generated content with viral potential. Is it possible to create a piece of digital information with the same kind of appeal as the two English brothers Charlie and Harry, but which also carries a commercial message that resonates with the chosen target audience? A number of branded viral marketing campaigns have actually been relatively successful, but they have generally been not just a simple video-clip released on the Internet but, rather, immersive multimedia productions intended to involve and activate the user in some way or another. An example of such a 'marketing campaign' was the alternate reality game launched by Nine Inch Nails and the advertising agency 42 Entertainment in 2007 (see Case study).

As Trent Reznor explained: 'The term "marketing" sure is a frustrating one for me at the moment. What you are now starting to experience IS "year zero". It's not some kind of gimmick to get you to buy a record – it IS the art form' (Marchese 2007). In other words, the game and the album should be considered as two equally important parts of an immersive multimedia experience. I recognize the parallels between Reznor's statement and the discussion regarding 'option value blurring' phenomenon in chapter 3, and conclude that, in the new music economy, the distinction between promotional material and the 'actual experience' is rapidly disappearing.

Audience-driven talent development

Perhaps the most important capability of a record label is to develop unpolished talents into professional entertainers and recognized brands. This capability comprises different components, such as financial resources, coaching skills, musical craftsmanship and the ability to see the potential superstars among the plethora of mediocre wannabes. At its core, components of the talent-development process remain the same in both the old and the new music economy. For instance, still the most important and common way to develop a talent is through extensive touring. It is on stage that young artists will slowly but surely develop a musical craftsmanship, learn how to interact with an audience and to appreciate the romantic ambience in a tour bus from 1982. However, the empowerment of the audience does make some dents in this area as well – for instance, in the financing of new talent development. Record labels usually invest in recording projects in the hope that they will eventually get a positive return on their investment. The money is needed for the actual recording and also for promoting the album to raise awareness and demand among prospective fans.

Cloud-based services, such as social network services, enable a completely different way of providing funding for music projects, or for any kind of project for that matter. The concept is known as 'crowd funding' and is best explained through an example. SellaBand.com, based in Munich, Germany, is a social network service that focuses explicitly on music and is a place for unsigned artists as well as music lovers to meet. The unsigned artists are able to upload their homemade demos for the music lovers to enjoy. Those music lovers who appreciate the work of an artist and want to hear more can invest in that artist. The investors buy what SellaBand.com calls 'parts' for $10 each, and as soon as 5,000 parts have been sold, the artist is assigned a producer and is given the opportunity to record a full-length album. Besides getting a CD for every part the investor owns, SellaBand.com has created a set of mechanisms that is supposed to provide incentives for the investors to promote the artist to their friends and the rest of the world. Among other things, the investors are given a share of the revenues from the adverts which are displayed on the SellaBand website.

There are other crowd-funding services that use slightly different models, but that also have been able to fund music-related projects of various kinds. The New York-based company Kickstarter runs one such general-purpose crowd-funding service. Kickstarter claimed that by 2012 it had raised more than $350 million from 2.5 million people to fund 30,000 projects. Although it is a general-purpose service, music-related projects constitute almost a third of all successfully funded projects and more than $50 million has been raised to fund them. One often-mentioned Kickstarter success story is Boston-based Amanda Palmer, who was able to raise close to $1.2 million for her music/art project from 24,800 fans.

Another aspect of the talent-development process affected by the evolution of Internet-based social network services concerns the arenas and the methods for spotting new talents. In the really old days, A&R agents spent their nights at shady clubs and minor venues in the hope of discovering a talent before the competition did. When the compact cassette, the CD-R and eventually the MP3 format made low-cost music storage and distribution available to unsigned artists, A&R agents were able to stay at their desks and listen to the loads of demos sent to their offices by hopeful musicians. These new technologies changed the decision-making process considerably, partly because the A&R agents increasingly based their talent-spotting decisions on a recording rather than on a live performance.

Social network services open up yet another arena for the A&R agents' talent-spotting activities. SoundCloud and other similar social network services allow unsigned artists (or creative consumers, if you prefer) to shortcut the A&R agent and present their own music directly to the other members of the network. Data and basic statistics describing how other users respond to the artist's music and image are able to support the A&R agents' decision-making. Such real-time market research data reduces the risk of overlooking talents which the audience loves but which the A&R agents are unable to recognize as artists with high potential.

The conflict between consumers and rights holders

From a strictly contractual perspective, the majority of creative and social music fans' activities are in breach of the stated conditions for using the content in question. The rights holders define the 'Terms of Use' in order to inform the audience what they can and cannot do without the holders' explicit permission. Usually, 'all rights' are reserved for the rights holder (cf. pp. 17ff), and the buyer of a music recording is not allowed to duplicate, lease or publicly perform or broadcast the song without explicit permission to do so. Similarly, music fans who, without explicit permission, upload a remix to their social network homepages, redistribute the song via email or file-sharing networks, or use the music to create new music videos are in breach of their agreements with the music firm. From a strictly contractual perspective, the music firm has the right to receive compensation for that unauthorized use and the potential damage they might have sustained.

However, often things are not as straightforward as that. While a successful court case might put a stop to a specific contractual breach and perhaps bring in some cash in the short term, it could have serious negative implications for the firm's business in the longer term. I have already discussed the importance of audience actions in raising media presence and promoting an artist. By discouraging fans from remixing and uploading music, music firms are, by definition, limiting this contribution to its media presence, which in turn has a negative impact on sales.

Another related problem is the link between the ability to control the distribution of an intellectual property and the consumers' ability to access that property. Based on previous discussions in this chapter, we know it is important to balance control and access. If control is limited, many consumers will be able to enjoy the recorded music but the music firm will have difficulties in generating any revenues from that use. On the other hand, if control is strict, only a few consumers will have access to the songs and will be able to learn to like them. In other words, a policy that implies that every contractual breach should be brought to trial would lead to a business performance below the optimal. The big question then is when to sue and when not to sue. There are several examples where rights holders have refrained from suing. For instance, in the case of the Britney Spears fan video discussed above, Philip Campbell Jr., the creator of the video, actually sent the piece to the record label, which, to this date, has not given its permission for it to be shown, but neither has it reacted negatively to the unauthorized use of its content. One might argue that, since the fan video was made without any commercial intentions and without trying to hurt the Britney brand, probably even the most narrow-minded record label would choose not to sue Mr Campbell. However, in general it is difficult to define any universal rules and routines for how a music firm should respond to copyright infringement.

I recognize that some of the music fans' activities are seriously hurting the music firms' businesses and probably deserve to be brought to trial by the rights holders. However, I also argue that social and creative music use is the normal way in which music fans use music in the new music economy. In other words, it is not consumers who are out of line and should be brought back into the corral; it is rights holders who need to rethink their terms of use. One viable way forward might be the licensing scheme suggested by the non-profit organization Creative Commons, founded by Lawrence Lessig in 2001. The general thinking behind Creative Commons licensing is to introduce some flexibility into the relationship between rights holders and consumers of culture. According to traditional copyright licences, 'all rights' are reserved to the rights holder. In contrast, if an intellectual property were licensed to a consumer by means of a Creative Commons licence, it would be possible to give the consumer 'some rights' – for instance, to redistribute an unaltered work for non-commercial purposes – while 'some rights' can still be reserved for the rights holder. Such a model would be considerably more in tune with the new music economy and would be better able to balance the needs of both rights holders and consumers of culture.

6

Future Sounds

In this book, I have laid out some of the most fundamental dynamics of the contemporary music industry. Based on this examination, I will in this last chapter sketch the contours of how the music industry may evolve in the future. It should be noted that the music industry is obviously as chaotic and unpredictable as any other complex dynamic system, and most attempts to make forecasts quickly become fairly ridiculous and futile. However, I believe it is indeed possible to explore, with some lasting relevance and value, at least some dimensions of future music industry development. In the first chapter I laid out the basic features of the new music industry dynamics and concluded that it is characterized by high connectivity and little control, music provided as a service and increased amateur creativity. I will now revisit these three features in an attempt to figure out what might be waiting around the corner.

Connectivity vs. control

The most important of the three features, actually underpinning the other two, is related to the tension between connectivity and control. I have argued that music firms have lost the ability to control how their music is distributed and used. However, as mentioned in the previous chapter, the battle between connectivity and control is far from over, as there are strong forces trying to limit the former and regain the latter. In recent years, we have witnessed how new copyright legislations have resulted in extended terms of copyright protection, harsher punishment for copyright infringers, better tools for rights holders to gather information about the use of their intellectual property, and so on.

These observations might lead you to believe that the current loss of control is only temporary. Rights holders will soon have regained full control of their intellectual properties and things will go back to normal. People will resume their old consumer habits and pay for the music they desire, and music companies will once again be able to invest in long-term talent development. However, there are two main reasons why this simply will not happen. First, a democratic and free society is based on the right to anonymity and the free flow of information, regardless of whether it is online or offline. The problem is that, online, it is difficult to control one kind of information and leave all other kinds alone. This means that any attempt to control online communication, regardless of good intentions, may have severe anti-democratic consequences, including the risk of creating a society where private communication is monitored and the free flow of information is impossible. Even though history shows us that democracy should not ever be taken for granted, I both hope and believe that this is a price which the societies I think of as democratic and free will be unwilling to pay.

The battle between connectivity and control has been going on for decades. Stewart Brand once famously explained:

> Information Wants To Be Free. Information also wants to be expensive. Information wants to be free because it has become so cheap to distribute, copy, and recombine – too cheap to meter. It wants to be expensive because it can be immeasurably valuable to the recipient. That tension will not go away. It leads to endless wrenching debate about price, copyright, 'intellectual property', the moral rightness of casual distribution, because each round of new devices makes the tension worse, not better. (Brand 1987: 202)

Even though this tension will never go away, the second argument for why things will not go back to normal concerns the changing character of this 'wrenching debate'. For decades, this battle has mainly been between law and technology. However, the 'connectivity side', which previously has been poorly organized and largely represented by faceless information-technological innovations, has slowly become an ideological force to be reckoned with. We have seen how new licence structures such as Creative Commons have gained ground, and how the Pirate Party (an anti-copyright European single-issue party) has been successful in regional, national and European parliamentary elections. But how did this change happen?

Manuel Castells' concept of the 'Internet Culture' may help to shed some light on the issue. The Internet was, and still is, shaped within a specific social environment with its specific cultural characteristics. Castells (2001) argues that those fundamental cultural values and beliefs that permeated the social environment in which the Internet was once invented still influence most online activities. The roots of the Internet can, to a great extent, be found in the academic and scientific world and, although the Internet outgrew its academic birthplace many years ago, 'the scholarly tradition of the shared pursuit of science, of reputation by academic excellence, of peer review, and of openness in all research findings' continue to colour the culture of the Internet (2001: 40).

The sharing of ideas and innovations, which is essential to the scientific community, is a practice that is equally essential in other related communities, such as the 'hacker community'.[28] Hackers cherish freedom above everything else – the freedom to create, access, change and distribute knowledge and information. The whole concept of being a hacker is based on the ability to work on a freely available software in order to improve it in some way, and then to share it with one's peers in a common pursuit to create a more perfect technological solution. This 'gift practice' is not only motivated by generosity but also the source of prestige, reputation and social esteem among the members of the community. The more creative and interesting solutions you share, the more prestige and reputation you gain (Castells 2001).

It is interesting to note that these values and beliefs, which were originally confined to the field of open-source software programming, have spread into the world of music, movies, books and most other kinds of digitizable culture. Richard Stallman (2002), one of the main characters in the hacker culture, has often debated the music business:

> We can make the computer network the musician's ally. Imagine a convenient way to send somebody a dollar anonymously through the Internet: some sort of digital cash. Imagine that every time you read a book or listen to a recording, it displays a box on the side of the screen, which says 'click here to send a dollar to the writer or to the band'. If you like the band or the book you will send that dollar sometimes.

Influential opinion-makers such as Stallman, currently president of the Free Software Foundation, and Lawrence Lessig, founder of Creative Commons, have been able to legitimize the criticism of the current copyright regime and have paved the way for a balanced ideological debate about the role of copyright in democratic societies. The battle between connectivity and control is no longer merely a battle between technology and law, but a serious political debate between politicians and members of parliaments around the world.

The new attention given to the copyright debate, combined with the potential severe societal implications of further tightening copyright legislation, lead to the conclusion that the steady development of ever stronger copyright legislation that we saw during the twentieth century is about to come to an end. I believe in the strength of our democratic institutions and hope that it will be difficult to tighten copyright legislation any further. Rather, I anticipate that, during the next couple of decades, copyright legislation will slowly but surely become increasingly balanced and flexible to the benefit of holders, makers and users of musical rights.

Context and content

One question that is often raised by music industry professionals is whether the recorded music business can ever survive without strong and tight copyright legislation. Will the consumer business for recorded music continue to exist? As was argued in chapter 3, it seems unlikely that the sale of individual songs or albums to consumers will be able to keep its historical position as the music industry's most important source of revenue. It is important to note that the consumer's diminishing willingness to pay for individual songs is not immediately caused by online music piracy. An even stronger influencing factor may come from different kinds of legitimate 'non-music' online services. Most consumer-oriented online services are free to use. They are often funded through advertising or some other kind of indirect revenue source. It seems to be very difficult to communicate to consumers that, while some services can indeed be sustained by advertising revenues alone, others cannot. Most consumers do not care whether the costs of producing high-quality journalism, movies or music sometimes are considerably higher than the costs of operating a webmail service or a social network service. Influenced by the values and beliefs of the 'Internet culture', many consumers expect that, online, information should always be free to access, change and share. These values constitute a colossal challenge for managers and executives, regardless of copyright industry, who try to monetize their content online.

This may have dire consequences for many copyright firms, since online revenues will basically be considerably lower than the corresponding revenues in the offline world. It still remains unclear who in the end will be willing to pay for high-quality journalism when the physical newspaper is gone. It is equally unclear how music companies will be able to finance long-term investments in talent development or complex and creative studio recordings without full control of the pricing and distribution of recorded music. Despite these apparently insurmountable problems, those consumer business models for recorded music that were discussed in chapter 3 will be unviable as long as rights holders insist on getting 'offline royalties' from online services. Advertising-based music services compete on the same ad market as every other online service, and the prices they are able to charge their advertisers are determined by that market and not by music rights holders. This means that there is a limit to the advertising revenues that online music services are able to procure, and there is equally a limit to the royalties they can pay to music companies without quickly going bankrupt. If rights holders do not accept this reality, they will end up with no consumer revenues instead of at least some.

It remains to be seen whether services such as Pandora, Spotify and the others that try to operate a revenue model that combines advertising revenues and subscription revenues are viable or not. At the time of writing, none of them is profitable and music industry pundits are eager to predict their demise. However, it is difficult to escape the fact that these services are popular, attracting millions of users and apparently able to respond to consumers' demand for a simple and legal music service. It is essential to note that Spotify's success is not primarily based on an extensive music catalogue, nor does it have fair and decent relationships with rights holders. The primary reason for its success is simply that the service's features and structure are superior to those of its competitors. Put in other words, Spotify's competitive advantage is context rather than content. In an environment where the basic musical content is available for free only 'two clicks away', it is quite difficult to compete with basic access to that same content. The music consumer's problem is not to access the content, it is how to navigate, manage and manipulate the music in the Cloud and on their digital devices. At the moment, most online music services aggressively try to enhance their contextual features, allowing their users to get sophisticated music recommendations, to listen to music together with their online friends and to access synchronized playlists on multiple devices. When looking into the future of online music services, it seems as if this development is only in its infancy. How about a music service that is constantly attuned to the user's release of pheromones? I would definitely pay a premium for such a service. Fantasies aside, during the coming decade, I hope and believe that a plethora of contextual music services (with fair and balanced rights holder agreements) will emerge that will answer to the diverse musical needs most users are still unaware they actually have.

Creativity as consumption

One such musical need which users have already discovered is the desire to be an active participant in the music-making process: either independently making their own music and sharing it with others or being part of their idols' and role models' creative processes. This book started out by presenting the case of Nine Inch Nails and how Trent Reznor provided tools and building blocks to his fans and encouraged them to play with the music and develop their own songs and remixes. Another artist who has developed a very close relationship with her fans is the London-based singer and songwriter Imogen Heap. During the production of Heap's latest album *Ellipse*, she regularly published a video blog in which she discussed the development of her musical ideas. Eventually she published 40 video episodes on YouTube during the two years the album was in production. In each episode she played pieces of her music, explained her thinking and asked for feedback. About 50,000 fans regularly followed the blog and commented on what they saw. Heap picked up these comments, entered into a conversation with her fans using different types of digital channels, such as Twitter and Facebook, and allowed the feedback to influence her creative process. I have pointed at several examples of how the distinction between promotion and distribution is blurred in the new music economy and I argue that Imogen Heap's Twittering, YouTubing, blogging and what-have-you are more than promotion for upcoming albums and concerts – these activities are all part of an immersive multi-platform Imogen Heap experience.

It is the combination of all the different pieces that enables her to build such a strong relationship with her fans and stimulate their demand for more twitters, more video blogs, more concert tickets and more music.

Imogen Heap and Trent Reznor are two artists who have been able to respond to their fans' creative desires. They have turned the fans' creativity into their own consumer proposition and have thereby been able to build a business with low churn and high ARPU (average revenue per user), to borrow terms from telecom operator lingua. Creativity as a mode of consumption has become increasingly common in most copyright industries, not only the music industry. In the videogame industry, many franchises are entirely based on user-generated content, but also in more traditional industries, such as news media, user creativity has become an ingrained part of the value proposition. Today it is as common for online news media companies to provide tools for their readers to comment on news articles and to upload their own images as it is to have a header and a byline.

This development calls for artists, musicians, producers and songwriters alike to question their musical as well as their business identities. What is the value they deliver to their consumers and their fans? Is the value really the music or is it perhaps something else? In the music industry of tomorrow, most of the value might very well be located in the tools and the building blocks which allow fans to gossip about their shared interest, to play and remix the sounds and the songs, and so on. If that is the case, what then does it mean to be a creative artist in the music industry? Who are your competitors? Perhaps the fiercest competition does not come from other comparable artists or bands, but rather from other platforms that are able to facilitate fans' creative expression and social interaction – platforms such as *World of Warcraft* or *Harry Potter*. If that is the case, is it even relevant to talk about a music industry at all?

Final words

This book has been about the music industry. I have examined how the industry has developed into its current state and I have shared some thoughts about how it may develop in the future. I have argued that music companies will not be able to regain control of their intellectual property and that online music services will compete with their contextual features, rather than with content exclusivity. I also suggested that music consumption based on user creativity means that the industry is entering a new competitive field where the competition is no longer restricted to other musical artists but includes all kinds of platforms facilitating fans' creative expression. These are all very significant changes that transform the logic and dynamics of the music industry. This transformation has, and will continue to have, far-reaching implications for the industry. It will force companies out of business, it will create yet unknown opportunities for inventive entrepreneurs, and it will change the creatives' and audiences' relationships with the music they love. But although the industry may change, it will not die. In spite of the turbulent times, the love for music will not fade, and great music will continue to give us goose bumps and euphoria. There will always be a demand to make and to listen to music, and, as long as this demand persists, there will be opportunities for organizations to connect creatives with sponsors, aggregators and audiences. Even when they all have moved into the Cloud.

Notes

1 *Ghosts I–IV* reached the number 2 spot on Amazon's list of top sellers, 29 April 2008.
2 It was in 1999 when Shawn Fanning, at the time a student at Northeastern University in Boston, MA, USA, developed the Napster software.
3 Cf. Bill Gates's vision of 'friction-free distribution' and 'friction-free capitalism' (Gates 1995).
4 The book was actually written while Horkheimer and Adorno were living in Pacific Palisades, California, but the research institute remained formally located at Columbia University.
5 Hesmondhalgh does not use the term 'interactive media', but, rather, a combination of the terms 'Internet industry', 'electronic publishing' and 'video and computer games'. I believe that the term 'interactive media' – or 'interactive leisure software', which is the term suggested by the British CITF – incorporates the terms suggested by Hesmondhalgh.
6 This is why marketing mechanisms such as reviews and ratings play important roles in the media consumers' purchasing process. Reviews and ratings provide some guidance that allows the consumer to make an informed decision even when it is difficult or impossible to get full access to the product before the actual purchase.
7 According to one trade organization (IFPI 2004b), 100,000 new albums were released in 2004, which equals more than 250 albums per day. If each album contains ten songs, and each song lasts for $3^1/_2$ minutes, more than 8,500 minutes of new music are released every day. This means that the avid consumer has to listen to at least six songs simultaneously, 24/7, to be able to keep up.
8 See p. 54, where the concept of the preselection system is applied to the music industry.
9 For instance, Live Nation Entertainment is listed on the most important stock exchange for media firms, the New York Stock Exchange (NYSE). Sony Music is owned by Sony and Universal

Music is controlled by Vivendi; both Vivendi and Sony are listed on the NYSE.

10   An algorithmic task is one in which the road to the solution is straightforward and obvious. A heuristic task has no predefined road to its goal. A heuristic task does not generally have a predefined goal either, but can end in many ways. An example of an algorithmic task is 'Make some muffins!'; an example of a heuristic task is 'Cure cancer!'.

11   A 'record label' is an organization that releases a certain form of music with a certain brand, such as Motown (soul/R&B), Blue Note (jazz) or Roc-A-Fella (hip-hop/rap). Major multinational music firms usually own and control several labels; EMI Music, for instance, controls more than 50 different labels across the world.

12   Industrial organization economics, or IO economics, is a field of economics that studies the strategic behaviour of firms, the structure of markets and their interactions.

13   The preselection system framework is discussed on p. 22.

14   Airplay is a technical term used in the radio industry to state how frequently a song is being played on a radio station. For example, a song that is played several times a day would be classed as receiving a large amount of airplay. The term is used in the same way regarding music video channels, to state how often a music video is being played.

15   The name 'Tin Pan Alley' was originally a reference to the sound made by many pianos all playing different tunes in this small area, producing a cacophony comparable to banging on tin pans.

16   The audience–media engine is a segment of the music industry feedback model (Wikström 2006, 2009).

17   A callback tone is the sound the caller hears when calling someone. A ringtone is the sound the called party hears when someone is calling her.

18   A master recording is an original recording from which copies may be made.

19   'Streaming' is a technique for distributing audiovisual media across the Internet. The advantage of streaming, compared to 'downloading', is that the user can start to look at or listen to a streamed video or song almost immediately after the transmission has been initiated, and does not have to wait until the entire data file has been downloaded to his or her computer.

20   The iPod was not actually pre-loaded with the music; rather, the bundle included (a) the music player and (b) a coupon that enabled the customer to download the entire U2 collection from iTunes at a significantly reduced price.

21 A more extensive case study of the US version of *Pop Idol* (*American Idol*) is given by Jenkins (2006: 59–92).

22 ie:music is a London-based management company representing Robbie Williams and a handful of other artists (http://ww.iemusic.co.uk).

23 In sound recording, dubbing is the transfer or copying of previously recorded audio material from one medium to another. Bootlegging is trafficking in recordings that the record companies have not commercially released and may or may not be legal. A 'mix tape' (commonly the two words are stuck together as mixtape) is a homemade compilation of songs recorded in a specific order, traditionally onto a compact cassette.

24 Online at: http://www.pro-music.org.

25 Online at: http://www.music-united.org.

26 See: http://www.hadopi.fr/.

27 Another example of the establishment's appropriation of this once underground phenomenon was MTV's show *Ultimate Mash-ups* launched in 2004.

28 Note the difference between 'hackers' and 'crackers'. 'Cracker' (not 'hacker') is the correct name for describing cyber criminals (e.g., Kevin Mitnick) who illegally break into corporate computer networks, sabotaging communications systems or spreading software (viruses, worms, etc.) aimed at damaging the property of law-abiding citizens and organizations.

References

Adorno, T.W. (1941). On Popular Music. *Studies in Philosophy and Social Sciences*, 9(1): 17–48.

Albarran, A.B., & Chan-Olmsted, S.M. (1998). *Global Media Economics – Commercialization, Concentration and Integration of World Media Markets*. Ames: Iowa State University Press.

Alderman, J. (2001). *Sonic Boom: Napster, MP3 and the New Pioneers of Music*. London: Fourth Estate.

Almqvist, K., & Dahl, C. (2003). *Upplevelseindustrin 2003, statistik och jämförelser*. Stockholm: Swedish Knowledge Foundation.

Amabile, T.M. (1996). *Creativity in Context*. Boulder, CO: Westview Press.

Amabile, T.M. (1998). How to Kill Creativity. *Harvard Business Review*, 76(5): 77–87.

Anderson, C. (2004). The Long Tail. *Wired Magazine*, 12(10): 170–7.

Anderson, C. (2006). *The Long Tail – Why the Future of Business Is Selling Less of More*. New York: Hyperion.

Angwin, J., McBride, S., & Smith, E. (2006). Record Labels Turn Piracy Into a Marketing Opportunity. *Wall Street Journal*, 18 October. Last accessed 14 February 2013 at: at: http://online.wsj.com/article/SB116113611429796022.html.

Ansoff, H.I. (1965). *Corporate Strategy*. New York: McGraw-Hill.

Argyris, C., & Schön, D. (1978). *Organizational Learning: A Theory of Action Perspective*. Reading, MA: Addison-Wesley.

Aris, A., & Bughin, J. (2005). *Managing Media Companies – Harnessing Creative Value*. Chichester, UK: John Wiley & Sons.

Attali, J. (1985). *Noise: The Political Economy of Music*. Minneapolis: University of Minnesota Press.

Bain, J.S. (1959). *Industrial Organization*. New York: John Wiley & Sons.

Baym, N. (2010). *Personal Connections in the Digital Age*. Cambridge, UK: Polity.

Barfe, L. (2004). *Where Have All the Good Times Gone? The Rise and Fall of the Record Industry*. London: Atlantic Books.

Barney, J. (1991). Firm Resources and Sustained Competitive Advantage. *Journal of Management*, 17(1): 99–120.

Barrett, C. (2007). Is There Gold at the End of *In Rainbows? Music Week,* 13 October: 12–13.

BBC News (2006). Police Hit Major BitTorrent Site. *BBC News Online,* 1 June. Last accessed 4 February 2013 at: http://news.bbc.co.uk/2/hi/technology/5036268.stm.

Billboard Magazine. 1948–2008.

BitTorrent (2012). *BitTorrent and µTorrent Software Surpass 150 Million User Milestone; Announce New Consumer Electronics Partnerships.* Corporate Press Release. BitTorrent Inc. Published 9 January. Last accessed 20 March 2013 at: http://www.bittorrent.com/company/about/ces_2012_150m_users.

Borland, J. (2005). Sony CD Protection Sparks Security Concerns. *CNet News.com,* 1 November. Last accessed 4 February 2013 at: http://news.com.com/Sony+CD+protection+sparks+security+concerns/2100-7355_3-5926657.html.

Boulding, K.E. (1968). *Beyond Economics.* Ann Arbor: University of Michigan Press.

Boulding, K.E. (1978). *Ecodynamics: A New Theory of Societal Evolution.* Beverly Hills, CA: Sage Publications.

Boulding, K.E. (1981). *Evolutionary Economics.* Beverly Hills, CA: Sage Publications.

Bradshaw, T. (2012). Spotify Doubles Number of Paying Users. *Financial Times,* 31 July. Last accessed 4 February 2013 at: http://www.ft.com/intl/cms/s/0/cdf16422-db2d-11e1-be74-00144feab49a.html.

Brand, S. (1987). *The Media Lab: Inventing the Future at MIT.* New York: Viking.

Brown, J., & Duguid, P. (1991). Organizational Learning and Communities-of-Practice: Toward a Unified view of Working, Learning, and Innovation. *Organization Science,* 2(1).

Brown, J.S., Collins, A., & Duguid, P. (1989). Situated Learning and the Culture of Learning. *Educational Researcher,* 18 (1): 32–41.

Bruck, C. (1994). *Master of the Game – Steve Ross and the Creation of Time Warner.* New York: Penguin Books.

Brulin, G., & Nilsson, T. (1997). *Läran om arbetets ekonomi – Om utveckling av arbete och produktion.* Stockholm: Rabén Prisma.

Brunner, R., & Brewer, G. (1971). *Organized Complexity.* New York: The Free Press.

Brynjolfsson, E., Hu, Y., & Smith, M.D. (2003). Consumer Surplus in the Digital Economy: Estimating the Value of Increased Product Variety at Online Booksellers. *Management Science,* 49(11): 1580–96.

Bukowsky, R., & Connor, T. (2005). Famed Hit Factory to Close: The Sound of Silence at Studio. *New York Daily News,* 4 February. Last accessed 14 February 2013 at: http://www.nydailynews.com/archives/news/famed-hit-factory-close-sound-silence-studio-article-1.604248.

Burnett, R. (1990). Concentration and Diversity in the International Phonogram Industry. PhD dissertation, Department of Journalism and Mass Communication, University of Gothenburg, Sweden.

Burnett, R., & Weber, R.P. (1989). Concentration and Diversity in the Popular Music Industry 1948–1986. Paper presented at 84th Annual American Sociological Association Conference, San Francisco, 9–13 August.

Byrne, D., & Yorke, T. (2007). David Byrne and Thom Yorke on the Real Value of Music. Wired, 16(1).

Carr, N. (2008). The Big Switch: Rewiring the World, from Edison to Google. New York: Norton.

Castells, M. (1996). The Information Age: Economy, Society and Culture. Vol. 1: The Rise of the Network Society. Oxford: Blackwell Publishers.

Castells, M. (2001). The Internet Galaxy. Oxford: Oxford University Press.

Caves, R.E. (2000). Creative Industries: Contracts Between Art and Commerce. Cambridge, MA: Harvard University Press.

CBO (2004). A CBO Paper – Copyright Issues in the Digital Media. The Congress of the United States, Congressional Budget Office, August.

Chan-Olmsted, S.M. (2006). Issues in Strategic Management. In A.B. Albarran, S.M. Chan-Olmsted & M.O. Wirth (eds.), Handbook of Media Management and Economics. Mahwah, NJ: Lawrence Erlbaum.

CISAC (2012). CISAC Annual Report 2011. Paris: International Confederation of Societies of Authors and Composers. Published 29 May.

Coase, R. (1937). The Nature of the Firm. Economica, 4: 386–405.

Cohen, W.M., & Levinthal, D.A. (1990). Absorptive Capacity: A New Perspective on Learning and Innovation. Administrative Sciences Quarterly, 35: 128–52.

Coleman, M. (2003). Playback: From the Victrola to MP3, 100 Years of Music, Machines, and Money. New York: Da Capo Press.

Crocker, S. (1969). Host Software. UCLA: Network Working Group, 7 April. Last accessed 4 February 2013 at http://www.ietf.org/rfc/rfc1.txt.

Cunningham, M. (1999). Good Vibrations: A History of Record Production, 2nd edn. London: Sanctuary Publishing.

Cunningham, S. (2005). Creative Enterprises. In J. Hartley (ed.), Creative Industries. Oxford: Blackwell Publishing.

Cyert, R.M., & March, J.G. (1992[1963]). A Behavioural Theory of the Firm. Englewood Cliffs, NJ: Prentice Hall.

D'Arcangelo, G. (2007). Active Listening: Social Identity in the New

Economy. Speech given at the San Francisco Bay Area Chapter of ACM SigCHI meeting, 13 May. Last accessed 4 February 2013 at: http://www. baychi.org/calendar/20070313.

DCMS (1998). *Creative Industries Mapping Document*, Department for Culture, Media and Sport (DCMS), London. Last accessed 14 February 2013 at: http://webarchive.nationalarchives.gov.uk/20100407120701/ http://www.culture.gov.uk/reference_library/publications/4740.aspx.

Delikan, M. D. (2010). *Changing Consumption Behavior of Net Generation and the Adoption of Streaming Music Services*. Master thesis in Business Administration at Jönköping University, JIBS. Last accessed 4 February 2013 at http://urn.kb.se/resolve?urn=urn:nbn:se:hj:diva-12519.

Denis, Corey (2008). *New Music Economy: Defined?*. Posted on the Pho email list, 13 May.

Denisoff, R.S. (1975). *Solid Gold: The Popular Record Industry*. New Brunswick, NJ: Transaction Publishers.

Denisoff, R.S. (1988). *Inside MTV*. New Brunswick, NJ: Transaction Publishers.

Dowd, T.J. (2000). Music Diversity and the US Mainstream Recording Market, 1955–1990. *Rassegna Italiana di Sociologia*, 41: 223–63.

Dowd, T.J. (2002). Introduction: Explorations in the Sociology of Music. *Poetics*, 30: 1–3.

Dowd, T.J. (2004). Concentration and Diversity Revisited: Production Logics and the US Mainstream Recording Market, 1940–1990. *Social Forces*, 82(4): 1411–55.

Edison Media Research (2003). *The National Record Buyers Study*, 3, 23 June.

eMarketer (2012). *Global Music – Tuning Into New Opportunities*. New York: eMarketer.

EMI (2002). *EMI/Mariah Carey Part Ways*. EMI Corporate press release, 23 January.

EMI (2004). *EMI Announces Steps to Further Strengthen its Business*. EMI Corporate press release, 31 March.

EMI (2008). *EMI Music and Papa Joe Records Announce Distribution Partnership*. EMI Corporate Press release, 12 May.

Enders Analysis (2003). *Piracy – Will it Kill the Music Industry?* March.

England, R.W. (ed.) (1994). *Evolutionary Concepts in Contemporary Economics*. Ann Arbor: University of Michigan Press.

Engström, A., & Hallencreutz, D. (2003). *Från A-dur till bokslut – Hårda fakta om en mjuk industri*. IUC Musik & Upplevelseindustri. December.

ExMS (2005). *The Export Performance of the Swedish Music Industry – An Update for the Year 2004*. Stockholm: Export Music Sweden.

Ferguson, D.A. (2006). *Industry-Specific Management Issues*. In A.B. Albarran, S.M. Chan-Olmsted & M.O. Wirth (eds.), *Handbook of Media Management and Economics*. Mahwah, NJ: Lawrence Erlbaum.

Fisher, F. (1961). On the Cost of Approximate Specification in Simultaneous Equation Estimation. *Econometrica*, 29: 139–70.

Florida, R. (2002). *The Rise of the Creative Class: And How It's Transforming Work, Leisure, Community and Everyday Life*. New York: Basic Books.

Forbes (2011). Top Earning Dead Celebrities. Published 25 October. Last accessed 4 February 2013 at: http://www.forbes.com/sites/dorothypomerantz/2011/10/25/the-top-earning-dead-celebrities/.

Forrester Research (2003). *Downloading Music Hurts Europe's CD Sales*. January.

Foster, J., & Metcalfe, J.S. (eds.) (2001). *Frontiers of Evolutionary Economics: Competition, Self-Organization and Innovation Policy*. Cheltenham, UK: Edward Elgar.

Freedman, D. (2003). Managing Pirate Culture: Corporate Responses to Peer-to-Peer Networking. *International Journal on Media Management*, 5(3): 173–9.

Frith, S. (1978). *The Sociology of Rock*. London: Constable.

Frith, S. (1983). *Sound Effects*. New York: Pantheon.

Frith, S., & Marshall, L. (eds.) (2004). *Music and Copyright*, 2nd edn. Edinburgh: Edinburgh University Press.

Gartner (2011). *Gartner Says Worldwide Online Music Revenue from End-User Spending Is on Pace to Total $6.3 Billion in 2011*. Published 8 November. Last accessed 4 February 2013 at: http://www.gartner.com/it/page.jsp?id=1842614.

Gates, B. (1995). *The Road Ahead*. New York: Penguin Books.

Gelatt, R. (1977). *The Fabulous Phonograph: 1877–1977*. New York: Collier.

Gerstner, L.V. (2002). *Who Says Elephants Can't Dance?: Leading a Great Enterprise Through Dramatic Change*. New York: HarperCollins.

Ghemawat, P. (1991). *Commitment: The Dynamics of Strategy*. New York: Free Press.

Gibbons, F. (2002). Robbie Williams Signs £80m Deal. *Guardian*, 3 October 2002. Last accessed 4 February 2013 at: http://www.guardian.co.uk/uk/2002/oct/03/arts.artsnews.

Giles, D., Pietrzykowski, S., & Clark, K.E. (2007). The Psychological Meaning of Personal Record Collections and the Impact of Changing Technological Forms. *Journal of Economic Psychology*, 28: 429–43.

Girard, A. (1981). A Commentary: Policy and the Arts – the Forgotten Cultural Industries. *Journal of Cultural Economics*, 5(1): 61–8.

Glassman, R.B. (1973). Persistence and Loose Coupling in Living Systems. *Behavioral Science*, 18: 83–98.

Goodman, F. (2008). Rock's New Economy: Making Money When CDs Don't Sell. *Rolling Stone Magazine*, 29 May. Last accessed 16 September 2008 at: http://www.rollingstone.com/news/story/20830491/rocks_new_economy_making_money_when_cds_dont_sell.

Graff, G. (2003). Rolling Stones Start Up The New Year With Ford. *Yahoo! Launch*, 6 January.

Gronow, P. (1983). The Record Industry: The Growth of a Mass Medium. *Popular Music*, 3: 53–77.

Gronow, P., & Saunio, I. (1998). *An International History of the Recording Industry*. London: Cassell.

Hallencreutz, D. (2002). Populärmusik, kluster och industriell konkurrenskraft. PhD dissertation, Department of Economic Geography, University of Uppsala, Sweden.

Hamel, G., & Prahalad, C.K. (1993). Strategy as Stretch and Leverage. *Harvard Business Review*, 71(2): 75–84.

Hamilton, D.B. (1953). *Newtonian Classicism and Darwinian Institutionalism: A Study of Change in Economic Theory*. Albuquerque: University of New Mexico Press.

Hansson, N. (2004). Kommentar: Tom Waits? Idol i TV4? Inte en chans!. *Dagens Nyheter*, 19 September.

Hartley, J. (ed.) (2005). *Creative Industries*. Oxford: Blackwell Publishing.

Hartley, J. (2007). The Evolution of the Creative Industries – Creative Clusters, Creative Citizens and Social Network Markets. In *Proceedings Creative Industries Conference, Asia-Pacific Weeks*, Berlin.

Hax, A.C., & Wilde, D.L. (2001). The Delta Model: Discovering New Sources of Profitability in a Networked Economy. *European Management Journal*, 9(4): 379–91.

Hesmondhalgh, D. (2002). *The Cultural Industries*. London: Sage Publications.

Hirsch, P.M. (1970). *The Structure of the Popular Music Industry*. Survey Research Center, Ann Arbor: University of Michigan.

Hirsch, P.M. (1972). Processing Fads and Fashions: An Organizational Set Analysis of Cultural Industry Systems. *American Journal of Sociology*, 77: 639–59.

Hirsch, P.M., & Fiss, P.C. (2000). Doing Sociology and Culture: Richard Peterson's Quest and Contribution. *Poetics*, 28: 97–105.

Hollifield, C.A. (2003). The Economics of International Media. In A. Alexander et al. (eds.), *Media Economics: Theory and Practice*. Mahwah, NJ: Lawrence Erlbaum.

Horkheimer, M., & Adorno, T. (1944). *Dialektik der Aufklärung – Philosophische Fragmente.* Published in English as *Dialectic of Enlightenment.* New York: Seabury, 1972.

Horowitz, B. (2006). Creators, Synthesizers, and Consumers. *Elatable*, 16 February. Last accessed 4 February 2013 at: http://blog.elatable. com/2006_02_01_archive.htm.

Hoskins, C., & McFadyen, S. (2004). *Media Economics.* Thousand Oaks, CA: Sage Publications.

Howkins, J. (2001). *The Creative Economy. How People Make Money from Ideas.* London: Allen Lane.

IFPI (2004a). *The Online Music Report 2004.* London: The International Federation of the Phonographic Industry.

IFPI (2004b). *The Recording Industry in Numbers 2004.* London: The International Federation of the Phonographic Industry.

IFPI (2007). *The Recording Industry in Numbers 2007.* London: The International Federation of the Phonographic Industry.

IFPI (2008). *The Digital Music Report 2008.* London: The International Federation of the Phonographic Industry. January.

IFPI (2010). *Recording Industry in Numbers. The Recorded Music Market in 2009.* London: International Federation of the Phonographic Industry.

IFPI (2012a). *Recording Industry in Numbers. The Recorded Music Market in 2011.* London: International Federation of the Phonographic Industry.

IFPI (2012b). *Digital Music Report 2012.* London: International Federation of the Phonographic Industry.

IFPI (2013). *Digital Music Report 2013.* London: International Federation of the Phonographic Industry.

IFPI Sweden (2013). *GLF's Statistics on Music Sales in Sweden. Full year, 2012: Music Sales up by 14 percent.* Published 18 January. Last accessed 14 February 2013 at: http://www.ifpi.se/wp-content/uploads/Music-sales-GLF-2012-ENGLISH.pdf.

Imfeld, C.J. (2004). Repeated Resistance to New Technologies: A Case Study of the Recording Industry's Tactics to Protect Copyrighted Works in Cyberspace between 1993 and 2003. PhD dissertation, University of North Carolina at Chapel Hill.

Informa (2012). The Adele Effect Hits Major-Record-Company Market Shares in 2011. Music & Copyright's Blog. Published 2 May. Last accessed 4 February 2013 at: http://musicandcopyright.wordpress.com/2012/05/02/the-adele-effect-hits-major-record-company-market-shares-in-2011/.

Ipsos-Reid (2002). *Digital Music Behavior Continues to Evolve.* February.

The Irish Times (2006). Pussy Power? *The Irish Times – The Ticket*, 23 June.

ITU (2011). *Key ICT Indicators for Developed and Developing Countries and the World*. Published 16 November. Last accessed 4 February 2013 at: http://www.itu.int/ITU-D/ict/statistics/at_glance/KeyTelecom.html.

Jenkins, H. (2006). *Convergence Culture – Where Old and New Media Collide*. New York: New York University Press.

Kaldor, N. (1972). The Irrelevance of Equilibrium Economics. *The Economic Journal*, 82: 1237–55.

Kapferer, J.-N. (2004). *The New Strategic Brand Management – Creating and Sustaining Brand Equity Long Term*, 3rd edn. London: Kogan Page.

Karlsson, D., & Lekvall, L. (2002). *Den ofrivillige företagaren*. Nätverkstan Kultur i Väst. March.

Katz, M. (2004). *Capturing Sound – How Technology Has Changed Music*. Berkeley: University of California Press.

Kealy, E. (1982). Conventions and the Production of the Popular Music Aesthetic, *Journal of Popular Culture*, 16: 100–15.

Keller, M. (2006). Sweden Pulls the Plug on Pirate Bay. *Los Angeles Times*, 1 June. Last accessed 14 February 2013 at: http://articles.latimes.com/2006/jun/01/business/fi-piratebay1.

Knight, J.A. (1998). *Value-Based Management*. New York: McGraw-Hill.

Korte, E. (2005). Panel discussion: Music for Images. [Korte was at the time VP Music Director at Saatchi & Saatchi, New York.] Midem Conference, Cannes, France, 25 January.

Laing, D. (2012). What's It Worth? Calculating the Economic Value of Live Music. *Live Music Exchange Blog*. Published 12 June. Last accessed 4 February 2013 at: http://livemusicexchange.org/blog/whats-it-worth-calculating-the-economic-value-of-live-music-dave-laing/.

Lave, J., & Wenger, E. (1991). *Situated Learning: Legitimate Peripheral Participation*. Cambridge: Cambridge University Press.

Levine, R., & Werde, B. (2003). Superproducers – They're Reinventing the Sound of Music, and the Music Industry. *Wired Magazine*, 11(10): 124–37.

Leyshon, A. (2001). Time-Space (and Digital) Compression: Software Formats, Musical Networks, and the Reorganisation of the Music Industry. *Environment & Planning A*, 33: 49–77.

Liebowitz, S. (2002a). Record Sales, MP3 Downloads, and the Annihilation Hypothesis. Working Paper, School of Management, University of Texas, Dallas. 22 August.

Liebowitz, S. (2002b). *Re-thinking the Network Economy*. New York: Amacom.

Lister, M., Dovey, J., Giddings, S., Grant, I., & Kelly, K. (2003). *New Media: A Critical Introduction*. London: Routledge.

Lorenz, H.-W. (1989). *Nonlinear Dynamical Economics and Chaotic Motion*. Berlin: Springer-Verlag.

Lowry, T. (2008). Look Who's Doing OK in the Music Business. *Business Week*, 4110(90).

MacQueen, H., Waelde, C., & Laurie G. (2007). *Contemporary Intellectual Property – Law and Policy*. Oxford: Oxford University Press.

Madonna.com (2008). Robyn to Support Madonna's 'Sticky & Sweet' Tour. Press release. 17 June.

March, J.G., & Olsen, J.P. (1976). *Ambiguity and Choice in Organizations*. Bergen: Universitetsforlaget.

March, J.G., & Simon, H.A. (1958). *Organizations*. New York: Wiley.

Marchese, D. (2007). Further Down the Spiral. *The Salon*, 16 March. Last accessed 4 February 2013 at: http://www.salon.com/2007/03/16/nine_inch_nails_2/.

Mermigas, D. (2006). Cable Must Draw Guns for New-Media Battles. *The Hollywood Reporter*, 18 April. Last accessed 18 April 2006 at: http://www.hollywoodreporter.com/thr/columns/mermigas.jsp.

Meyer, J., & Rowan, B. (1978). The Structure of Educational Organizations. In M. Meyer (ed.), *Environments and Organizations*. San Francisco, CA: Jossey Bass.

Miège, B. (1979). The Cultural Commodity. *Media, Culture and Society*, 1: 297–311.

Miles, R.E., & Snow, C.C. (1978). *Organizational Strategy, Structure and Process*. New York: McGraw-Hill.

Miles, R.E., Snow, C.C., Meyer, A.D., & Coleman, H.J. (1978). Organizational Strategy, Structure and Process. *Academy of Management Review*, July: 546–62.

Millard, E. (2006). Music Industry Files 2,000 More Lawsuits. *Newsfactor Magazine Online* 4 April.

Mitchell, G. (2005). Prince of a Deal. *Billboard Magazine*, 117(52): 20.

Mjøs, O.J. (2012). *Music, Social Media and Global Mobility: MySpace, Facebook, YouTube*. London & New York: Routledge.

Moorefield, V. (2005). *The Producer as Composer: Shaping the Sounds*. Cambridge, MA: The MIT Press.

Myrdal, G. (1956). *Development and Under-Development: A Note on the Mechanism of National and International Economic Inequality*. Cairo: National Bank of Egypt.

Negus, K. (1992). *Producing Pop – Culture and Conflict in the Popular Music Industry*. London: Arnold.

Negus, K. (1996). *Popular Music Theory*. Cambridge: Polity.

Negus, K. (1997). The Production of Culture. In P. du Gay (ed.), *Production of Culture/Cultures of Production*. London: Sage Publications.

Nelson, R., & Winter, S. (1982). *An Evolutionary Theory of Economic Change.* Cambridge, MA: Harvard University Press.

Neuman, W.R. (1991). *The Future of the Mass Audience.* Cambridge: Cambridge University Press.

New York Times (2008). In Rapper's Deal, a New Model for Music Business. 3 April.

O'Connor, J. (2000). *Cultural Production Strategy.* Information for Cultural Industries Support Services, Manchester.

Oberholzer, F., & Strumpf, K. (2005). The Effect of File Sharing on Record Sales: An Empirical Analysis. Working Paper, Harvard Business School and University of North Carolina at Chapel Hill. June.

OECD (2005). *Working Party on the Information Economy, Digital Broadband Content: Music.* Organization for Economic Co-operation and Development, Directorate for Science, Technology and Industry, Committee for Information, Computer and Communications Policy. 8 June. DSTI/ICCP/IE(2004)12/Final.

Olin-Scheller, C., & Wikström, P. (2009). *Författande fans.* Lund: Studentlitteratur.

Oram, A. (ed.) (2001). *Peer-to-Peer: Harnessing the Power of Disruptive Technologies.* Sebastopol: O'Reilly Media.

Orwall, B. (1995). Purple Drain. *Saint Paul Pioneer Press*, 15 January.

Ouchi, W. (1978). Coupled versus Uncoupled Control in Organizational Hierachies. In M. Meyer (ed.), *Environments and Organizations.* San Francisco, CA: Jossey Bass.

Page, W. (2011). Wallet Share. *PRS for Music: Economic Insight* 22. Published 18 April. Last accessed 4 February 2013 at: http://www.prsformusic.com/aboutus/policyandresearch/researchandeconomics/.

Parrack, D. (2008). Rolling Stones Leave EMI for Universal – Follow Radiohead, McCartney Out the Door. *Brit Music Scene*, 26 July. Last accessed 4 February 2013 at: http://www.britmusicscene.com/rolling-stones-leave-emi-for-universal-follow-radiohead-mccartney-out-the-door/.

Peoples, G. (2012). Business Matters: Is Spotify Labels' #2 Source of Revenue? Probably Not. *Billboard.biz.* Published 27 June. Last accessed 4 February 2013 at: http://www.billboard.biz/bbbiz/industry/digital-and-mobile/business-matters-is-spotify-labels-2-source-1007443752. story.

Perrow, C. (1986). *Complex Organizations.* New York: Random House.

Peterson, R.A. (1976). *The Production of Culture.* Beverly Hills, CA: Sage Publications.

Peterson, R.A. (1979). Revitalizing the Culture Concept. *Annual Review of Sociology*, 5: 137–66.

Peterson, R.A. (1982). Five Constraints on the Production of Culture: Law, Technology, Market, Organizational Structure and Occupational Careers. *Journal of Popular Culture*, 16: 143–53.

Peterson, R.A. (1985). Six Constraints on the Production of Literary Works. *Poetics*, 14: 45–67.

Peterson, R.A. (1994). Culture Studies Through the Production Perspective. In D. Crane (ed.), *The Sociology of Culture: Emerging Theoretical Perspectives*. Cambridge, MA: Blackwell.

Peterson, R.A. (2000). Two Ways Culture is Produced. *Poetics*, 28: 225–33.

Peterson, R.A., & Berger, D. (1975). Cycles in Symbol Production: The Case of Popular Music. *American Sociological Review*, 40: 158–73.

Picard, R.G. (2002). *The Economics and Financing of Media Companies*. New York: Fordham University Press.

Picard, R.G. (ed.) (2005a). *Media Product Portfolios – Issues in Management of Multiple Products and Services*. Mahwah, NJ: Lawrence Erlbaum.

Picard, R.G. (2005b). Unique Characteristics and Business Dynamics of Media Products. *Journal of Media Business Studies*, 2(2): 51–9.

Picard, R., & Wikström, P. (2008). *Determinants of Domestic Music: An Empirical Analysis*. Presented at the 8th World Media Economics and Management Conference, Lisbon, Portugal.

Pine, B.J., & Gilmore, J.H. (1998). Welcome to the Experience Economy. *Harvard Business Review*, July–August: 97–105.

Poe, R. (1997). *Music Publishing: A Songwriter's Guide*, 2nd edn. Cincinnati, OH: Writer's Digest Books.

Porter, M.E. (1980). *Competitive Strategy: Techniques for Analyzing Industries and Competitors*. New York: Free Press.

Porter, M.E. (1990). *The Competitive Advantage of Nations*. London: Macmillan.

Porter, M.E. (1991). Towards a Dynamic Theory of Strategy. *Strategic Management Journal*, 12: 95–117.

Power, D. (2002). 'Cultural Industries' in Sweden: An Assessment of their Place in the Swedish Economy. *Economic Geography*, 78(2): 103–28.

Power, D. (ed.) (2003). *Behind the Music – Profiting from Sound: A Systems Approach to the Dynamics of the Nordic Music Industry*. Nordic Council of Ministers, Nordic Industrial Fund, Center for Innovation and Commercial Development.

Qualen, J. (1985). *The Music Industry: The End of Vinyl*. London: Comedia.

Radzicki, M.J. (1990). Institutional Dynamics, Deterministic Chaos, and Self-Organizing Systems. *Journal of Economic Issues*, 24(1): 57–102.

Radzicki, M.J., & Sterman, J.D. (1994). Evolutionary Economics and System Dynamics. In R.W. England (ed.), *Evolutionary Concepts in Contemporary Economics*. Ann Arbor: University of Michigan Press.

Read, O., & Welch, W.L. (1976). *From Tin Foil to Stereo: Evolution of the Phonograph*. Indianapolis, IN: Bobbs-Merrill and Howard W. Sams.

Reca, A.A. (2006). Issues in Media Product Management. In A.B. Albarran, S.M. Chan-Olmsted & M.O. Wirth (eds.), *Handbook of Media Management and Economics*. Mahwah, NJ: Lawrence Erlbaum.

Resnikoff, P. (2012). Why Spotify can't be Happy with 4 Million Subscribers. *Digital Music News*. Published 31 July. Last accessed 4 February 2013 at: http://www.digitalmusicnews.com/permalink/2012/120731spotify.

Reuters (2006). Swedish Police Shut Web Site in Music Piracy Raid. Reuters, 31 May. Last accessed 4 February 2013 at: http://news.cnet.com/Swedish-police-shut-Web-site-in-music-piracy-raid/2010-1030_3-6078588.html.

Reznor, T. (2012). Facebook Wall Post, 21 September. Last accessed 4 February 2013 at: https://www.facebook.com/photo.php?fbid=3265399 533874&set=a.3265399493873.108202.1833868712&type=1.

Rosen, C. (1994). Paisley Park, Warner Bros. Terminate Joint Venture. *Billboard Magazine*, 106(7): 5–6.

Sandvine (2012). *Global Internet Phenomena Report 2H 2012*. Waterloo, Ontario, Canada.

Schnur, S. (2005). Panel discussion: Music for Images. [Schnur was at the time World Wide Executive of Music at Electronic Arts.] Midem Conference, Cannes, France, 25 January.

Schumpeter, J. (1911). *Theorie der wirtschaftlichen Entwicklung*. Published in English as *The Theory of Economic Development: An Inquiry into Profits, Capital, Credit, Interest, and the Business Cycle*. Cambridge, MA: Harvard University Press, 1934.

Schumpeter, J. (1942). *Capitalism, Socialism and Democracy*. New York: Harper.

Scott, A.J. (1999). The Cultural Economy: Geography and the Creative Field. *Media, Culture and Society*, 21: 807–17.

Senge, P. (1990). *The Fifth Discipline*. London: Century Press.

Shapiro, C., & Varian, H.R. (1999). *Information Rules*. Boston, MA: Harvard Business School Press.

Simon, H.A. (1971). Designing Organizations for an Information-rich World. In M. Greenberg (ed.), *Computers, Communications and the Public Interest*. Baltimore, MD: Johns Hopkins University Press.

Simon, H.A. (1979). *Rational Decision-Making in Business Organizations*. Stockholm: The Nobel Foundation.

Simon, H.A. (1981). *The Sciences of the Artificial*. Cambridge, MA: MIT Press.

Simon, H.A., & Ando, A. (1961). Aggregation of Variables in Dynamic Systems. *Econometrica*, 29: 111–38.

Smith, E. (2007). Madonna Heads for Virgin Territory; Concert Promoter

Lures Material Girl From Warner Music With $120 Million. *Wall Street Journal*, 11 October.

Stalk, G. (1988). Time – The Next Source of Competitive Advantage. *Harvard Business Review*, 66(4): 41–51.

Stalk, G., Evans, P., & Shulman, L. (1992). Competing on Capabilities. *Harvard Business Review*, 70(2): 57–69.

Stallman, R. (2002). Let's Share! *www.openDemocracy.net*, 30 May. Last accessed 25 February 2003at: www.openDemocracy.net.

Sterman, J.D. (1994). Learning in and about Complex Systems. *System Dynamics Review*, 10: 291–330.

Stock, M. (2004). *The Hit Factory: The Stock, Aitken and Waterman Story*. London: New Holland Publishers.

Suhr, H.C. (2012). *Social Media and Music: The Digital Field of Cultural Production*. New York: Peter Lang.

Svenska Dagbladet (2004). Såpor skapar inte stjärnor. *Svenska Dagbladet*. 7 September.

Tapscott, D., & Williams, A. (2006). *Wikinomics: How Mass Collaboration Changes Everything*. New York: Penguin.

Teece, D.J., Pisano, G., & Shuen, A. (1997). Dynamic Capabilities and Strategic Management. *Strategic Management Journal*, 18(7): 509–33.

Thompson, H.S. (1988). *Generation of Swine: Tales of Shame and Degradation in the '80s*. New York: Simon & Schuster.

Thorburn, D., & Jenkins, H. (eds.) (2003). *Rethinking Media Change: The Aesthetics of Transition*. Cambridge, MA: The MIT Press.

Thorselius, R. (2003). *The Look for Roxette*. Stockholm: Premium Förlag.

Throsby, D. (2001). *Economics and Culture*. Cambridge: Cambridge University Press.

Towse, R. (2001). *Creativity, Incentive and Reward: An Economic Analysis of Copyright and Culture in the Information Age*. Cheltenham: Edward Elgar.

Toynbee, J. (2000). *Making Popular Music – Musicians, Creativity and Institutions*. London: Arnold.

Varian, H. (1979). Catastrophe Theory and the Business Cycle. *Economic Inquiry*, 17: 14–28.

Vogel, H.L. (2001). *Entertainment Industry Economics*, 5th edn. Cambridge: Cambridge University Press.

Wallis, R. (1995). The Future of Radio as Seen from the Outside. *Nordicom-Information*, 1995(1): 11–23.

Wallis, R. (2004). Copyright and the Composer. In S. Frith, & L. Marshall (eds.), *Music and Copyright*, 2nd edn. Edinburgh: Edinburgh University Press.

Watts, D.J. (2003). *Six Degrees: The Science of a Connected Age*. New York: Norton.

Weber, M. (1921). Die rationalen und soziologischen Grundlagen der Musik. Published in English as *The Rational and Social Foundations of Music*. Carbondale, IL: Southern Illinois University Press, 1958.

Weick, K. (1976). Educational Organizations as Loosely Coupled Systems. *Administrative Science Quarterly*, 21: 1–19.

Wenger, E. (2006). *Communities of Practice – A Brief Introduction*. Last accessed 4 February 2013 at: http://www.ewenger.com/theory/commu nities_of_practice_intro.htm.

Wernerfelt, B. (1984). A Resource-based View of the Firm. *Strategic Management Journal*, 5(2): 171–80.

Wikström, P. (2005). The Enemy of Music – Modelling the Behaviour of a Cultural Industry in Crisis. *The International Journal on Media Management*, 7(1 & 2): 65–74.

Wikström, P. (2006). *Reluctantly Virtual – Modelling Copyright Industry Dynamics*. PhD dissertation, Media and Communication Studies, Karlstad University, Sweden.

Wikström, P. (2009). The Adaptive Behaviour of Music Firms – Introducing the Music Industry Feedback Model. *Journal of Media Business Studies*, 6(2): 67–96.

Wikström, P., & Burnett, R. (2009). Same Music, Different Wrappings. *Popular Music and Society*, 32(4): 507–22.

Wildman, S.S. (2006). Paradigms and Analytical Frameworks in Modern Economics and Media Economics. In A.B. Albarran, S.M. Chan-Olmsted & M.O. Wirth (eds.), *Handbook of Media Management and Economics*. Mahwah, NJ: Lawrence Erlbaum.

Witt, U. (2003). *The Evolving Economy – Essays on the Evolutionary Approach to Economics*. Aldershot, UK: Edward Elgar.

Wolf, M.J. (1999). *The Entertainment Economy*. London: Penguin Books.

Yeaman, N. (2008). En kvinnlig Ziggy Stardust. *Dagens Nyheter*, 22 August.

Zaid, G. (2003). *So Many Books: Reading and Publishing in an Age of Abundance*. Philadelphia, PA: Paul Dry Books.

Index